TURN YOUR IDEAS INTO MONEY

TURN YOUR IDEAS INTO MONEY

by
Donald W. Cantin

HAWTHORN BOOKS, INC.
PUBLISHERS / *New York*

Library of Congress Catalog Card Number: 72-2141
ISBN: 0-8015-7996-1

Design by STAN DRATE

3   4   5   6   7   8   9   10

TO
JEANNIE
. . . the best idea I ever had

Foreword

You are holding the most comprehensive book ever written on the subjects of creation, protection, and marketing of ideas. Its premise is a simple one: Everyone in the world gets ideas at one time or another, but relatively few people know how to go about presenting them to potential buyers. With this book you will learn that the power of ideas, properly applied, is the most valuable force on earth. This information could literally change your life.

There is no magic or mystery in turning ideas into money. There are no secrets you cannot learn. There *are* time-proven methods and techniques you can follow successfully: The basic knowledge and steps you must take are clearly outlined in these pages.

This is a serious business study for people of imagination and ambition. There are no "get-rich-quick" schemes here; no empty inspirational pap; and no "case histories" as filler material. Everything you need to know in taking the first step toward making money from your ideas is between these covers—the rest is up to you.

The author's first concern is to make you realize that the world of trade and commerce is concerned primarily with one thing: *ideas*. New companies were started on ideas. Old dying companies were brought back to life because of ideas. Investors provide financial help to people with ideas. Consumers are motivated to buy through ideas. Audiences pay to be entertained by ideas.

Donald W. Cantin is highly qualified to author this book: He has spent his life in the business of "selling ideas" as an advertising and marketing expert for some of the biggest companies in the world. Among his clients have been Clorox bleach, United Vintners (The Little Old Winemaker), the Bank of California, Cutty Sark scotch, Helena Rubinstein, Stridex, Fruit of the Loom, Medi-Quik, Protein 21 shampoo, and countless others.

If you're tired of sitting on your ideas, this is your chance to act.

NEIL RANSICK
President
American Trends, Inc.
New York City

Contents

Are You the Type? . . . What Are Your Chances
for Success? . . . How Much Capital Will You
Need? . . . Should You Share Ownership with
Others? . . . Where Should You Locate? . . .
Should You Buy a Going Business? . . . Are
You Qualified to Supervise Buying and Selling?
. . . How Will You Price Your Products and
Services? . . . What Selling Methods Will You
Use? . . . How Will You Manage Personnel? . . .
What Records Will You Keep? . . . What Laws
Will Affect You? . . . What Other Problems
Will You Face?

A Part-time Beginning . . . Who Buys by Mail
and Why . . . Criteria for the Selection of Merchandise . . . Sources of Supply . . . Developing
a Clientele . . . Rules and Regulations . . . Adequate Records . . . Materials Available

Sample Letters . . . Release Forms

TURN YOUR IDEAS INTO MONEY

Introduction to the World of Ideas

An idea is not the exclusive property of the "ivory tower" intellectual, nor is the ability to create something new restricted to recognized or self-styled geniuses. There is nothing mysterious about an idea. Powerful and profitable ideas can, and do, occur to *everyone* at one time or another. Sometimes a great idea will come about "automatically," without apparent effort. At other times the most concentrated and diligent endeavors will bring about only weak and questionable results.

There are three important considerations involved in the creation of any idea: (1) the individual and his experiences, (2) the environment and the stimuli it provides, and (3) the transactions and interactions between the individual and the stimuli. Regardless of the process or method involved, be it conscious effort or subconscious inspiration, ideas will "happen."

The main object of this book is to help insure that ideas, once they are born, are not wasted and forgotten simply because their originators did not know what to do with them—did not know how to take the steps necessary to translate ideas into money.

Even the best idea in the world is worth absolutely nothing when it is sitting in the back of someone's mind. For an idea to have any value, it must be made tangible and must be communicated to others. Only then can it reward its owner. It was once said: "Nothing happens in this world until someone first has an idea." Look around you and see how true this is: Manufacturing, publishing, advertising, designing, marketing, buying and selling, could not exist until the first step had been taken—the idea.

An idea is the most valuable thing in the world and should be treated as such. It must be well cared for, protected, and communicated carefully.

The book you are holding was once only an idea. So was your automobile, your pencil, your home, and the television programs and commercials you watched last night. Everything was once only an idea: the ax, the paper clip, children's toys, the design of your clothes, and advertising slogans. Nature itself has been subjected to man's application of ideas. A tree is certainly not man's idea, but the selling of Christmas trees or a variety of trees at commercial nurseries was man's idea. Weather and climate, certainly not the works of man, are being sold by man at famous resorts around the world.

An idea, then, to have commercial value, must have three parts: (1) the concept itself, (2) a plan or purpose of action, and (3) the execution of that plan. Most people stop at the first phase, the idea it-self, and never go any further. You've met these peo-ple. Whenever they see a new product idea, they say, "I had that same idea months ago!" These are the same people who see television programs and commercials and offer an idea of their own, or an im-provement, which they claim could do a better job for the sponsor. However, these people never do any-thing about their ideas.

Discretion and research are almost as important as the idea itself. Not all ideas are great ideas. Some are hopelessly bad and can't even be given away. It is necessary that ideas be evaluated for their merit before any attempt is made to sell them. Moreover, judgment must be exercised when offering to sell an idea. What may be worthwhile to one manufacturer or television network or advertising agency may be worthless to another.

Another important factor to consider: The sale and success of an idea can often be 90 percent dependent on its presentation. An idea offered for sale must be "packaged" properly, as with anything that is offered for sale. A postcard to a manufacturer seldom makes a sale. An idea worthy of the name must be pre-sented with drama and excitement. It must have pro-fessional sizzle.

Whether an idea is scientific or artistic, preparing for its sale must be approached in a rational and businesslike manner. Not everyone realizes this, yet *everyone* is involved in the business of selling: the poet who sells his literary expression; the politician who sells his ability to represent the people of his community; every employee selling his services to his employer.

Selling is not difficult if certain techniques and procedures are followed. You must have something worth selling; you must know whom to sell it to; and you must do it professionally. There is more on these subjects in later chapters.

Now let us consider for a moment how ideas occur. Your own experience will confirm the fact that ideas happen primarily in three very distinct and definable ways: consciously, subconsciously, and by accident.

The Conscious Effort

Through conscious effort and application you deliberately seek an idea because you either *have* to or *want* to. Having to produce an idea falls in the category of "problem-solving"; you are faced with a situation that requires an "idea solution," and you consciously and systematically attempt to find one or more answers that will eliminate that problem.

Prehistoric man knew that walking over rough terrain bruised and damaged his bare feet, that hot rocky ground burned him in the summer, and that winter cold and snow were even worse. He thought about this and eventually reasoned that it wasn't necessary for his feet to come into contact with the ground if he simply wrapped a piece of animal hide around each foot.

With the passing of years (and centuries) this early solution to a problem underwent many changes and embellishments: sandals, boots, shoes, high heels (invented by the Persians to keep their feet off the hot desert sand), roller skates, ice skates, showshoes, spiked shoes for sportsmen, weighted shoes for deep-sea divers, magnetic shoes for astronauts, and a recent invention, buoyant shoes for walking on water.

Most of these developments came about because someone had a particular need that had to be satisfied. When the fisherman wanted to wade deeper into the stream he was fishing, he modified existing boots by making them longer and thus had the idea for hip boots. This conscious effort to solve a problem prompted the saying: "Necessity is the mother of invention."

Wanting to produce an idea need not necessarily be linked to problem-solving. That is, an actual recognized *need* may not exist prior to the idea itself; there may not be a pressing problem to be solved. In other words, the only *need* present is to *want* to produce an idea. Scientific or artistic mental exercise often produces such ideas, some of which may have no immediate application.

Leonardo da Vinci had the original idea for the helicopter, not because he needed one, but merely to explain the laws of physics upon which he was speculating. His idea preceded by hundreds of years the engineering knowledge necessary to build it.

This area of ideas whose existence does not derive from a real "problem-need" is often vague and difficult to isolate and label. The idea for a best-selling novel certainly does not derive from the reading public's need for the novel, and it may not derive from the author's need to communicate a particular message or philosophy.

The idea for a new breakfast-food package design or feature, intended for consumers whose need for it is so small it couldn't be measured, may have originated at an advertising-agency brainstorming session whose purpose for meeting may have been the general production of ideas for any of their clients. There need not have been any specific need to solve a marketing or advertising problem.

The Subconscious at Work

Not all ideas come about because someone has to or wants to have an idea. Setting out to produce ideas sometimes produces nothing of value, if anything at all. We'll never know how many ideas were not the result of deliberate effort but were instead a "gift" from the subconscious. The phenomenon of the creative process is at its most dramatic and startling when it seems to happen by itself. In fact, ideas "out of the blue" may sometimes be frightening in their suddenness.

When ideas occur to you unpredictably, almost as if it were against your will (or at least without your will), the work of your subconscious mind has broken through to the conscious level of your mind. It is a curious process: You may awaken in the middle of the night with an idea to solve a problem you hadn't thought about in weeks or years; you may be in the middle of a conversation with a friend and be struck with an idea which is in no way related to the conversation.

What is happening on the subconscious level of

your mind is the same thing that happens on the conscious level, except that it usually cannot be controlled. The subconscious works in its own strange and sometimes devious ways and at its own speed. Moreover, it often seems to exercise a high degree of judgment and efficient selection.

Ideas from the subconscious are often very sound and reasonable, almost as if the unworkable ideas had been eliminated or prevented from reaching the conscious level. Perhaps this is one reason why this type of idea is often called inspired.

Whether it is called subconsciousness, fringe consciousness, or preconsciousness, it is there, and it can be put to work in almost the same way as the conscious mind, although the results may not always be predictable. This will be investigated in the next chapter.

Accidental Discovery

The third way ideas come about is through "lucky accidents," whereby ideas discover themselves. These require only that someone be around to observe these "accidents" and that someone be equipped to understand and act upon them. The word *serendipity* means accidental discovery. Horace Walpole suggested the word after reading "The Three Princes of Serendip," a fairy tale. As the princes traveled, they continually made "discoveries, by accident or sagacity, of things they were not in quest of." Serendipity may not always be the exact word in this case: Some idea men are in quest of an "idea solution" through hard work and experimentation but find their answer to a problem accidentally.

Alexander Graham Bell and Thomas Watson would not have invented a way to transmit and receive vocal sounds over wire when they did if the make-and-break points of a transmitter spring had not accidentally become welded together. This accident was understood by them and led to the invention of the telephone ten months later.

William Kelly's discovery of refining molten pig iron into wrought iron or steel by forcing oxygen through the molten mass to reduce its carbon content was the result of an accidental observation, which he was able to understand. Henry Bessemer, an Englishman, later discovered the same thing accidentally and developed a more sophisticated method to do the same work, and the process was named after him. Another example is Hans Christian Oersted's discovery of the relation between electricity and magnetism.

When these and similar accidents occurred, the observers were qualified and had the experience to comprehend what was happening and were able to perfect the accident into a meaningful discovery. It was Louis Pasteur who said, "In the field of observation, chance favors only the minds which are prepared."

It must be remembered that *any* idea could be salable and profitable. Whether the idea came into life because there was a critical need for it, whether someone simply sat down and concentrated on producing free-wheeling ideas, whether an idea was

subconscious inspiration, or whether it was the result of accident, ideas are ideas, and the good ones
are worth money.

Nothing is so powerful as an idea whose time has
come.

CHAPTER 2

How to Create and Develop Salable Ideas

You are reading this book because you are a person who gets ideas and realizes that they are worth money. Knowing this, you should now be asking yourself some very important questions: If ideas can be sold, wouldn't I have a better chance of making money if I could create—manufacture—as many ideas as I wanted? The answer is Yes. The more ideas you have, the better the odds on having a truly valuable idea.

Next question: Is it possible for me to increase my ability to produce ideas? Some people almost never get an idea, whereas others seem to turn them out like link sausage—one after another. Again the answer is Yes. Creating ideas is a function of the mind, like anything else we do—driving a car, typewriting, swimming—and the more effort, practice, and experience that go into it, the easier it becomes.

The secret of creating ideas is in learning how to

deal with and control the mental process that performs this unique task. This process of idea-making can be understood, can be controlled, and can be made to work for you.

Quite a lot of work has been done by many competent people in formalizing the idea-making process. Most of this work was done with a view to explaining it, however, and not in showing how it could be utilized.

Accidental Discovery

W. B. Cannon in his article "The Role of Chance in Discovery" (*Scientific Monthly*, Vol. L, 1940) suggested that accidental discovery occurs not only when something new is observed, but also when a new relevance is involved in the observation, whether it is new or old. "In order to be prepared for this, two conditions are necessary: A) a knowledge of the past . . . since this knowledge enriches the meaning of present experience, and B) an open mind . . . an ability to weigh ideas on their merits and judge them fairly and critically."

F. C. McLean, the scientist, has said: "Accidental discovery comes most often to the man who has given much conscious thought to the problem upon which he is engaged and who is in a position to grasp, through both conscious and unconscious mental processes, the significance of any accidental observations he may make. This accidental discovery is most apt to come to the scientist who makes the greatest use of his facilities, including those of rational analysis."

It is, of course, also clear that accidental discovery occurs only when the scientist is actively at work. The operative word here is "work," and it wouldn't be presumptuous to suggest that the points made by McLean apply equally to fields of endeavor other than science.

The Subconscious

In his book *The Art of Thought* (New York: Harcourt, Brace, 1926) G. Wallas had many important things to say about the subconscious thought process. He suggested that there were four stages in the formation of new thought: (1) preparation—investigation of the problem; (2) incubation—the stage when the individual is not consciously thinking of the problem; (3) illumination—when the idea occurs; and (4) verification—when the idea is tested and reduced to exact form.

Wallas also recommended disciplinary habits which could facilitate the art of thought, such as arranging time for intellectual work; preceding actual work with a warming-up period by thinking about the task; not becoming upset if work is slower on some days than others; having a specific plan to work; noting down scattered ideas in a folder, notebook, or file; marking the passage of a book when an idea occurs while reading.

Wallas warned that the individual should be master, and not the slave, of his habits. "Without industry great intellectual work cannot be done, yet mere industry may prevent creation."

Conscious Effort

Among the better contributions to the study of creative thought has been the work of Alexander Osborn. His book, *Applied Imagination* (New York: Charles Scribner's Sons, 1953), provides valuable insights into the idea-making process. Osborn believed that persons could be trained to improve their use of imagination and offered suggestions to enrich their creative powers, such as the accumulation of first-hand experiences, as in travel, hobbies, solving puzzles, reading, and writing.

His greatest contribution was his theory that the creative process, without following any rigid sequence, consists of some or all of the following phases: (1) orientation—pointing up the problem; (2) preparation—gathering up pertinent data; (3) analysis—breaking down the relevant material; (4) hypothesis—piling up alternatives by way of ideas; (5) incubation—letting up to invite illumination; (6) synthesis—putting the pieces together; (7) verification—judging the resultant ideas. These phases are an expanded version of Wallas's work.

With this review and understanding of the creative and idea-making process the next step is to formalize this information and arrange it into a pattern which can be of some use in evaluating the ideas you already have, in improving them, and in creating more and better ideas. We now have enough background information to start working. We can distill all that we have learned and formulate an idea-making method—a method that will work for both your conscious mind and your subconscious mind and will even prepare you for accidental discovery.

The Idea Method

The idea-making method involves the basis of all creative and constructive ideas: the recombination of all known elements from past experiences and current stimuli. If you have an objective in mind, the method can teach you to put two thoughts together to produce a third, which hopefully will be new and valuable. Operation of the method requires these three factors:

1. *The Idea Subject.* This is the focal point of the operation. It can, and often does, represent the problem that must be solved or the basic area of consideration against which the application of ideas would be desirable. In the case of the prehistoric man, mentioned earlier, the Idea Subject would be his *feet.*

2. *The Tangible Goal.* This factor represents the desired result—not the idea itself, but what the idea is expected to do. To continue our prehistoric-man example, the Tangible Goal would be *the elimination of discomfort* to his feet.

3. *The Creative Stimulus.* This third factor is that which, when applied to the Idea Subject, prompts

the creation of an idea. More than one Creative Stimulus may be needed to prompt a worthwhile idea.

The operation of the Idea Method is simple. Keeping the Tangible Goal in mind, creative stimuli are applied to the Idea Subject. In the case of our prehistoric-man illustration, creative stimuli were very likely applied in a haphazard and undirected manner. Our cliff dweller probably did not have the sophistication required to control any kind of systematic thought process, yet, in his own crude way, and without knowing it, he experienced an event very similar to the method here presented. First, he was aware of the Idea Subject: his *feet*. Second, he realized his Tangible Goal: *the elimination of discomfort* to his feet. When it came to creative stimuli, however, he was at a disadvantage. His sources for stimuli were extremely limited when compared to the present day. His backlog of experience was not large or varied, and his primitive environment did not offer much stimulation. Yet, consciously or unconsciously, all of the factors above were present in his situation and somehow combined to give him his idea solution.

Perhaps the stimuli of wild animals around him suggested that he walk on hands and knees or like the monkeys, swing from branch to branch in the trees. These were idea solutions but bad ones. Birds flying overhead may have prompted the thought that he try flying, but he probably regretted his attempt. The comfort of his cave may have been the stimulus that gave him the idea not to go out at all; this may have been temporary comfort to his feet but again was not the best solution. We can only speculate on how long he must have sat pondering his cold and bruised feet before his eyes fell upon the animal skins in the far corner of his cave and gave him the stimulus he needed.

Let's examine how this idea-making method, which has always existed, can be used to make money in this modern-day world.

The Idea Subject can be anything at all—a piece of machinery, a book, a consumer product, a chemical, a toy, a philosophical approach, a radio program —any element that can interest you and can function as a focal point for the operation of the method.

The Tangible Goal is what you *want* from the operation of the method. It could be an improvement in a piece of machinery, a more worthwhile book, a more convenient consumer product, a new chemical compound, and so on. It may happen that the Tangible Goal is more "goal" than "tangible." That is, you may simply want to produce a new and salable idea but have no particular need or specific objective in mind.

The Creative Stimulus is the most important factor. We've seen that this is usually provided by the mind's recall of past experiences or by our immediate environment. The method hinges on the application of this factor but does not rely on the mind's ability to recall, which can be faulty, nor on the environment, which can often be more distracting than helpful.

The secret of the method is in the application of *controlled, semiabstract, symbolic, artificial stimuli.* A listing of these is presented later in this chapter with suggestions as to how they can be used. Although dozens of these stimuli are offered, you'll soon realize that you will be able to construct many more on your own—ones that may prove to be more valuable, workable, and comfortably familiar to you. This will become easier when you understand that they are intended to substitute, by means of the printed word, for your past experiences and those of others, and for today's environment.

To illustrate with something closer to home than a caveman's foot wrappings, let's assume you are concerned with a mechanical device—say, an ordinary door lock—your Idea Subject. Your Tangible Goal could have one or more parts: to improve it, to increase its sales to the public, to make it less expensive to produce. Now, all that remains is to take the three factors above and run them through a listing of creative stimuli, such as is provided later in this chapter.

You'll run through quite a few that will have little or no value, such as *Audience participation, Direct mail, Make a gift version, Dramatize, Lengthen,* and *Make it hotter,* before you find one or more that you can use, such as *Miniaturize.* Does miniaturization offer anything in connection with door locks? What happens if we make smaller door locks?

First of all, a smaller door lock is less expensive to produce, because it requires less raw material, and thus increases profits by reducing manufacturing costs. With lower production costs the manufacturer may decide to pass these savings on to his customers by lowering the price. The law of supply and demand tells us that lower prices can result in increased sales.

What are the other benefits of this idea? Smaller door locks would weigh less than those of conventional size, and shipping costs might be reduced considerably, another saving worth money. Smaller door locks would mean smaller keys, an important consideration for people who dislike carrying many of the heavy, bulky keys necessary today. This would be a unique product distinction which would allow for competitive advertising claims.

This same system will work with any Idea Subject. The typewriter was made *portable* and *electric;* books were made in *three dimensions* in braille for the blind, and "talking books" came about when someone thought to *add sound;* cigarettes were made *safer* with the addition of filters; milk was *repackaged* in cardboard containers, which were *disposable;* detergents are sold with *free premiums* in them; chemicals are *combined* to produce new formulas; children's toys are more *realistic* and made with *less expensive* plastics; some television programs are done *on location;* advertising is becoming more specialized and effective by the use of *ethnic* appeals.

People have been having ideas for years, and they will go on having them. With the Idea Method, you can have ideas at will.

Creative Stimuli

Put it horizontal, vertical	Video tape
Guest stars	Make it larger
Interview	Photography
Transistorize	Outer space
Why status quo?	Foreign sales
Audience participation	Expand distribution
Add sound	Quiz
Appeal to emotions	Have a series
Edit	Change price
"His and hers"	Stunts
Henry Ford	Plug it in
Aerate	Make it 3-D
Emboss, die-cut, gatefold	Tie in with . . .
Research	Make it smaller
Investigate, survey	Assemble, disassemble
Test, use	Timeliness

Repetition	Do it faster
Style	World, universe
Truth	Ethnic groups
Make it heavier	Combine
Nation, continent	Project
Do it slower	Divide
Go on location	Make it sour
Testimonials, endorsements	Decorate
Add danger	Chart, diagram, map
Liquefy	Habit, fad, custom
Remove sound	Make it safer
Make it lighter	Legalities
Showmanship	Make a model
Look to the future	Emphasize
Solidify	Add a part
Change of pace	Remove a part
Mark Twain	Business trends

Maximum	Initial it
Birth, life, death	Reverse, mirror
Make it sweet	Make it look like something else
Make it obsolete	"Mister [product, brand]"
Albert D. Lasker	Be literal
Disassemble	Zipper, tape
Streamline	Give it texture
Reissue	Romance
Fantasy	Gauge, measure, meter, scale
Translate	Origin of product, service,
Weather	name
Change a part	Participation
Music, voice	Motorize it
Minimum	Vice versa
Make a set	Calendar
American sports	Put on floor, wall, ceiling
Foreign sports	Break up a set

Animate

How to . . .

Push button, lever, handle

Stretch, shrink

Snob appeal

Henry Miller

Finance

Trial and error

Symbolism

Hobbies

Make square things round

Offer: premium, sample, trial

    coupon, contest, service

Change color

Repackage

Frank Lloyd Wright

Make it hotter

Date for freshness

Recognizable

Have a team

Make it two-dimensional

Holidays

Transportation

Subconscious need

Antonym, synonym

Folklore, magic

Make it stronger

Summer, fall

Security, health, power

Themes

Make it colder

Parade

Cut, paste, staple, bind

News value

Male, female, child, infant

Reproduce in other media

Darwin

Graphics

Legend, superstition

Competition

Make it weaker

Winter, spring

Spectacular

Direct mail

Sketch, doodle

Attention, interest

Foreign markets

Parody, lampoon, satire

Complaints, pet peeves

Make it adjustable

Mystery

Make it opaque

Rhinestones

Show business

Dictionary, glossary

Thesaurus, directory

Put it on an ocean, mountain

Consult experts

Confucius

Demand, action

Animals

Change direction

Sophisticate

Interchangeable

Make it transparent

Lincoln

Meat and produce

Catalog, index, guide

Almanac, checklist	Curiosity
Bibliography	Edsel
Put it on the farm	World travel
Advertise	Make it realistic
Make a gift version	Dramatize
Publicize	H. G. Wells
Glamorize	Co-op
Optical effects	Guarantee
Automation	Birthdays
Advisory board	Telephone
Oddities	Rolling thunder
"Take one"	War
Optical illusion	Match color to use
Limited: offer, time, quantity	Da Vinci
Synthesize	Lengthen
Reproduce in other material	Revive, repeat history
Shorten	Human interest

Sports

Religion

Brand names

Cartoons

Place in other situation

"National [product] Week"

Display

Mats

Follow-up

Fee, commission

Family

Use actual things

Influential groups

Make it more expensive

Day-Glo, fluorescence

Make it compact

Inventory

Patent, copyright

Place in other environment

Self-service

Career

Exaggeration

Powderize, pulverize

Competition

Different container

Odorize (add, remove, change)

Make it less expensive

Quick-freeze

Make it portable, collapsible

Go to extremes

Miniaturize

Put it in the city, the air

Conventions, meetings

Backward, forward

Sex	Customize
Education	Code
Efficiency	Alphabet
Clubs, organizations, societies	Gambling
Reusable package	Make a "junior" size
Make a giant size	Make a line of related products
Summerize it	Reduce the line to one product
Winterize it	Relate it to the gay 90's
Personalize it to buyer	Run a contest to dramatize
Use it as a prize	Tie in with Santa Claus
Make it disposable	Inert ingredients
Charity	Tie in with store promotions
Put it in the dark	Study successes
Trade shows, exhibits	Repeat, repeat, repeat
Sideways, up, down	Nothing is impossible

A few final remarks: As soon as possible, make up your own list of creative stimuli. Use your judgment in evaluating the ideas you produce. Ask yourself if there is a benefit connected with the idea—who would buy it? Don't forget research. The best idea in the world can't be sold by you if someone else owns it.

You needn't work alone if you have a compatible partner—one you can trust. Each of you could stimulate the other, and the combined experiences and intellect might produce more than twice the number of ideas both of you could produce working alone.

Warning! Sometimes an idea, a great idea, will come to you with so little effort you might think that it is obvious to everyone. Someone, somewhere, you may think, must have thought of it before you. Don't make that mistake! Giving up and discarding an idea because it came to you easily is the most dangerous thing you can do. All ideas appear simple and obvious *after* someone has had them. Guard your ideas, protect them, value them. Never sell them short.

Selling Advertising Ideas

It isn't necessary to be an advertising expert in order to have a valuable advertising idea, but some knowledge of the business and how it operates would be helpful to anyone trying to sell that idea.

The responsibility for most of the advertising you see today rests with advertising agencies. Their function is to create ads—messages to the consumers about the advertisers' products or services. The agencies then recommend to their clients the best way to communicate this message—television, magazines, direct mail, etc. After their recommendations are accepted, they buy space or time in the various media.

Agencies also offer collateral services, such as research, packaging, and merchandising. Not all advertising is placed through advertising agencies. Some companies, such as retail stores, may have their own advertising departments or rely on the local newspaper for assistance.

The people connected with advertising deal in high-priced projects and are serious and cautious professionals well able to judge upon the merits of an idea. They deal with ideas for a living. Rather than frighten or deter you from attempting to approach these people, this should encourage you. Good ideas will be recognized, and the better your ideas, the more money they will be worth.

In learning how to sell your advertising ideas, you should know and understand the many types and categories that exist. You may find that one idea can be used in many areas and in many ways. These are the categories with which you should familiarize yourself:

1. *Copy ideas:* Copy is the foundation of advertising and is the primary method used to communicate a selling message to the consumer. The effective use of language, whether spoken or printed, is a valuable talent. New and unique ways of putting words together are worth money.

This includes your ideas for rewriting advertisements so they will be better understood; it includes your ideas for emphasizing an important product feature that the agency or advertiser may not be aware of; it includes your idea for a rememberable slogan, catch-phrase, rhyme, or product name; it includes almost everything.

2. *Art ideas:* These are ideas that are visual and can be reproduced on television and in magazines, newspapers, displays, or other print media. Art includes photography; drawings and paintings; typography; the layout, composition, and design of ads;

direction of film commercials; and all related endeavors such as set decorations and costuming.

3. *Aural ideas:* These are ideas that relate to the sense of hearing and can involve the use of music, sound effects, vocal effects, singing, and jingles.

These three basic types of advertising ideas, and their combinations, can be employed in almost two dozen basic ways and in hundreds of variations. Keep your ideas in mind when reviewing the list that follows; you'll see that they increase in value as the many different manners of using them become apparent.

1. *Television:* network, local, black and white, color, international (via satellite), live, video tape, film, ethnic stations and programs, UHF, VHF, educational.

2. *Newspapers:* morning, evening, weekly, daily, Sunday, foreign, use of color, inserts, home delivery, mail, subscription.

3. *Magazines:* general, sport, fashion, teen, women's, men's, regional, trade, business, foreign, color, gatefolds.

4. *Direct mail:* mail-order selling, salesmen's leads, gimmicks, contests, coupons, order forms, incentives, bounce-backs, referrals, circulars, broadsides, throwaways.

5. *Outdoor advertising:* painted boards, spectaculars, three-dimensional boards, posters, signs, illuminated, motion, dirigibles, skywriting, tri-vision.

6. *Transit advertising:* bus and subway cards, taxi cards, airline, train, terminal.

7. *Business publications:* export-import, trade papers and magazines, house organs, professional publications.

8. *Point of purchase:* window displays, floor and counter displays, shelf, overhead, illumination, motion, sound.

9. *Farm publications:* national, regional, agricultural types.

10. *Religious publications:* denominational, clergy, faith.

11. *Exhibits:* conventions, street, shopping center, trade, parade floats, consumer.

12. *Sampling:* personal, in-store, home, mail, random, advertising offer, free, reduced cost.

13. *Selling aids:* manufacturer, distributor, wholesaler, salesmen, retailer.

14. *Catalogs:* brochures, order blanks, want books, mail order, store order desk.

15. *Premiums:* with/without product, for sale, giveaway, mail-in, specialized.

16. *Film:* industrial film, trade shows, theater screen.

17. *Novelties and specialties:* matchbooks, pens and pencils, ashtrays, calendars, wallets, books, key chains, etc.

18. *Retail promotions:* supermarkets, movie houses, service stations, shopping centers, contests, sweepstakes, loss leaders, giveaways, demonstrations.

19. *Miscellaneous:* theater programs, telephone directories, etc.

Whom to Sell To

Advertising Agencies

In one sense, advertising agencies are your first and best potential buyers because they serve a number of different client advertisers. Your idea may be useful to the agency itself or to more than one client advertiser. Reaching all of these buying prospects with one letter makes your selling job easier. Agencies, because they deal with ideas on a daily basis, will immediately be able to recognize the value of your idea and its possible application.

However, selling to advertising agencies is easier said than done: Of all the "idea categories" covered in this book, selling advertising ideas is the most difficult. The great majority of agencies, particularly the larger ones, are extremely reluctant to view ideas submitted by persons outside of their organizations. Many agencies have adopted a policy of not considering any ideas whatsoever from outside sources. The reason for this policy is basically legal protection.

Because of the abstract nature of advertising ideas, it is very difficult (and sometimes impossible) to establish ownership and origination. It is likely that you could submit an idea identical or very similar to one the agency has been working on. Therefore, many agencies would rather risk not learning of your possibly valuable ideas than spend their time and money in court to settle any dispute or misunderstanding with you.

Despite this strong policy, some agencies *do* listen to outside ideas, and they *do* have release forms which they will ask you to sign for their protection before looking at your ideas. You can break through this policy held by many agencies of not looking at outside ideas and get to the point where you will be asked to sign a release form in these ways:

1. Write a strong first letter. (See Chapter 12, Exhibit B.)

2. Write to more than one person at each agency in an attempt to generate interest in your idea. (Sources listed later in this chapter will give you the names and titles of agency personnel.)

3. Try to reach potential buyers through personal contacts and mutual friends.

4. Don't be afraid to use the telephone to ask for a personal interview.

Remember: Never disclose your idea in a first letter or in a telephone conversation. Read and study Chapters 7, 8, and 9 on protection.

You might find that your idea for a specific type of business doesn't interest agencies who have clients in that business. In that case you can write to other agencies and suggest to them that the idea might be useful to them in obtaining clients in that business.

Depending on your personal circumstances, you might consider "selling your ideas" by offering your services as an *employee*, perhaps as a full-time or part-time copywriter, art director, or marketing consultant.

Write directly to the president of the agency, the chairman of the board, the vice-president in charge of creative services, the creative director, the account supervisor or account executive, or any of the personnel in the sources given later in this chapter whom you feel are appropriate. If your idea has to do with research, media, or merchandising, write to the appropriate department or to the vice-president.

In Chapter 12 you will find sample "first letters" to advertising agencies and typical release forms, contracts, and letters of agreement that you might be asked to sign if the agencies are interested in hearing your ideas.

At most libraries you will find a reference book entitled *Standard Directory of Advertising Agencies* (Skokie, Ill.: National Register Publishing Co., Inc.). This book lists thousands of advertising agencies, including branches. Approximately half of the list also includes the clients handled by the agencies. The listing is cross-referenced alphabetically and geographically. There are also other similar books and trade publications available which can give you this information.

THE ADVERTISERS

Whether or not you are able to interest the advertising *agencies,* you can always write directly to the advertiser *companies* themselves. For some ideas it is likely that you will get a better reception than from the agencies. Then, too, the odds are better of your making a sale. There are more manufacturing and service companies than there are advertising agencies.

Your best prospects, of course, would be those

companies who already have a product or service that could benefit from your idea, but don't ignore the companies in related fields or industries. Your idea could give them the opportunity they have been seeking to expand their business and branch out.

Here, too, you should write to the president, chairman of the board, the vice-president in charge of advertising, or the advertising director. Depending on the nature of your idea, you might wish to write to the marketing director or the manager of the New Products Division.

All large libraries have a reference source of prospects called *Standard Directory of Advertisers* (Skokie, Ill.: National Register Publishing Co., Inc.). This is a classification of nationally advertised articles and services, the company itself, and the mailing address. Principal executives and the advertising managers are listed, as well as the advertising agency handling the account, the account executive in charge, and the media used. The data is cross-referenced alphabetically and geographically, by lines of business, trademark, and advertising agencies. Another source to check at your library is *Thomas Register of American Manufacturers.*

Other Possible Buyers

Advertising agencies and advertisers aren't the only places where you can sell your ideas. There are thousands of other businesses connected with advertising which deal with ideas to the same extent.

1. *Television-commercial companies:* produce the films and video tapes for the advertising agencies. Look up *Television Fact Book,* published by *TV Digest,* 2025 I Street, Washington, D.C. 20006, and *Broadcasting Yearbook,* Broadcasting-Telecasting Building, 1735 De Sales Street N.W., Washington, D.C. 20006, at your local library, or write directly to them.

2. *Radio production companies:* make the recorded advertisements on tapes or disks. You can learn where these companies are by checking the sources above, as well as *Film/Tape Semi-Annual Source Book,* published by *Television Age,* 1270 Avenue of the Americas, New York, New York 10020.

3. *Typographers:* set up the printing type for advertisements. Your first source here is the yellow pages. Then contact the Society of Typographic Arts, 18 South Michigan Avenue, Chicago, Illinois 60603, and the International Typographic Composition Association, 303 Washington Building, Washington, D.C. Each of these associations has a monthly publication and might be able to put you in contact with some of their members.

4. *Photographers:* whose work appears in print media. Contact the American Society of Magazine Photographers, 1472 Broadway, New York, New York 10036, and ask for their directory of members. Another source is the Professional Photographers of America, 152 West Wisconsin Avenue, Milwaukee, Wisconsin 53203.

5. *Outdoor and transit advertising companies:* sell advertising space and often produce the advertisements you see on billboards and signs and on some

vehicles. Your best source for these companies is *Standard Rate and Data,* a trade publication available at your library, categorized by advertising medium.

6. *Artists and art services:* Artists do the work; art services perform the selling function, as do artists' representatives. Your source here is *Literary Market Place* (R. R. Bowker Company, 1180 Avenue of the Americas, New York, New York 10036), available at your library or bookstore.

7. *Direct-mail houses:* handle all the details and merchandising of an advertising campaign conducted through the mails. Contact *Direct Marketing Magazine,* 224 Seventh Street, Garden City, Long Island, New York. Also at your library.

8. *Novelty and specialty manufacturers:* supply agencies and advertisers with these items, as well as contest prizes, awards, business gifts, etc.

9. *Promotion, contest, and premium firms:* originate, adapt, and sell their products or ideas to agencies, advertisers, and even to companies that don't advertise.

10. *Point-of-purchase display producers:* construct and often create the placards, signs, and illuminated and motion displays seen in stores.

Good sources for the last four categories are *Buyer's Guide* and a business magazine called *Advertising and Sales Promotion,* 740 Rush Street, Chicago, Illinois 60611. After checking your local yellow pages, contact Advertising International, 520 North Michigan Avenue, Chicago, Illinois 60611, and the Point of Purchase Advertising Institute, 11 West 42nd Street, New York, New York 10036.

You should consider that the ideas you can offer for sale to these businesses can be of two types: ideas for the businesses themselves and ideas for advertisers which these businesses can help you develop and sell. Although the preceding list is made up primarily of suppliers, they are often the originators of ideas and have experience in selling them and putting them to work. Your letter to these suppliers should be patterned after the approaches used for advertising agencies and advertisers (see Chapter 12).

In your first contact with these businesses, the subsequent correspondence, and any personal contact, remember that ideas are the stock in trade of advertising people and that they are basically in the idea-presentation business. You should prepare your own idea story and presentation so that it will be worthy of the people you are talking to. Be professional and businesslike. Bear in mind the benefits of your idea, and don't let your emotions carry you away. Remember, too, that your ideas will be competing with the ideas of the agencies' own copywriters, artists, and idea men. Don't forget the importance of research mentioned earlier.

CHAPTER

4

Selling Television and Radio Program Ideas

The television and radio industry requires an almost constant infusion of new ideas. Programs remain on the air only as long as they are successful in attracting and holding their listening and viewing audiences. If they fail to do this, they are replaced by new programs.

The television and radio stations themselves are not the origin of all that you see and hear broadcasted. Thousands of people not directly employed by the networks and local stations make contributions to broadcasting, and they are paid quite respectable sums of money for them. Writers and idea men, who provide the essential raw material from which programs are made, are held in special regard by broadcasters. This is where you come in.

Program ideas fall into two basic categories: dramatic and nondramatic.

Dramatic programs come in all forms: tragedy,

comedy, western, love, crime, war, philosophical, mystery, and so on. There are original stories and adaptations of successful books or short stories. Some are fifteen minutes in length, others one hour, and still others two hours or more.

Nondramatic programs have as broad a range and include: children's, educational, quiz and game, interview/conversation, public service, and "specials" of one kind or another.

If you have an idea for any one of these types of programs (or perhaps for a *new* type) and it is a *good* idea, you can sell it. The question is, How do you go about it?

You can submit your idea in many ways. If it is a dramatic program, you can write a complete script, you can prepare a comprehensive outline of the story idea, or you can submit a one-paragraph synopsis. If your idea is for a continuous weekly series, you might write two scripts and eleven outlines, giving you a package of thirteen programs—enough for a "thirteen-week" broadcast cycle (one quarter of a year).

Generally speaking, completed scripts will be better received than outlines or synopses. A finished idea in proper form is easier to sell than the outline of that same idea. However, outlines of dramatic programs have sold in the past, and they will continue to sell in the future. Writing ability is important, and quality writing has a value of its own, but anything written must proceed from an idea—a concept—and concepts stated in one sentence have been sold.

Your understanding of this is especially important

if your idea is for a nondramatic program. You can write a script for a documentary program or a variety show, but if your idea is for a weather program, a conversation/interview show, or a news program, you will have to submit it as a descriptive outline.

In Chapter 13 you will find suggested reading material which will give you sample radio and television scripts, outlines, and synopses.

Whom to Sell To

NETWORKS

Television and radio networks are the best customers for programming ideas, but by no means the only ones. These companies are continually seeking new properties and will give your submissions every attention. Very likely you will find that they will ask you to sign release forms before looking at your work. Although these forms will be forwarded to you automatically when you first write, you can save time by requesting them in advance and in this way also learn how they prefer your idea be submitted to them.

You might find a few (very few) networks or stations who will refuse to look at your work unless you are an established writer. If you run into this, you'll learn that there are other ways to get your idea on that network by reading below.

When submitting your idea, you will be writing to the Story Department, Program Department, program development director, or other appropriate department or person. You will find the addresses of all major radio and television networks and stations in *Standard Rate and Data* at your local library.

LOCAL STATIONS

There are two important points with regard to the sale of ideas to local broadcasting stations: (1) Many, if not most, ideas for national network programs cannot be sold to local stations simply because the independent stations do not have adequate production facilities, budgets, or personnel. (2) Not all radio and television ideas are suitable for nationwide viewing or listening on the networks. Many programs, by nature, can be shown only regionally and must originate with the local stations.

Local stations might prove to be excellent prospects for your ideas, particularly those that fall in the nondramatic category. While your compensation is not as great, neither is your competition from other writers and idea men.

ADVERTISING AGENCIES

In the programming area agencies function as intermediaries between the networks or local stations and the sponsoring companies. In acting as agents for the advertisers, they often get deeply involved in the selection and production of programs. In many cases the advertising agencies are the sources of program ideas. By coordinating between their clients and the broadcast media, they are sometimes the most influential factors in carrying an idea through to its execution.

Use the *Standard Directory of Advertising Agencies* mentioned previously for your sources, and write to the creative director, the programming director, or anyone listed with appropriate title.

ADVERTISING SPONSORS

In addition to trying for sales to the broadcasting companies and advertising agencies, you should consider the advertising sponsors of broadcast programs as possible buyers. These companies, after all, provide the money that makes the programs possible. Not only are they sometimes influential in determining which programs go on the air, they are often directly involved in the actual production, including the selection of writers and performers.

You would write to the vice-president in charge of advertising, the advertising director, or the advertising manager. Use the *Standard Directory of Advertisers* mentioned in Chapter 3 as your source for this category.

MOTION PICTURE COMPANIES AND INDEPENDENT PROGRAM PRODUCERS

These represent a large and excellent market for your ideas. Working alone or in cooperation with the networks, these companies produce almost all of the national programs that are seen on television. To the programs, you can add all of the motion pictures that are leased to the television broadcasters. As a rule, these companies will not look at unsolicited manuscripts and ideas. Most sales are made through agents or directly by established writers, but there is no law preventing you from writing to these companies. Radio production companies are not great in number but are more likely to give your work a hearing.

Literary Market Place, at your library, is a good source for this category as well as for agents, covered below.

AGENTS

If you have past sales to your record, you will have no trouble in obtaining an agency to represent you and sell your literary efforts. If you haven't yet sold any broadcast ideas and/or manuscripts, you will have to write to a number of agents outlining what you have in mind or send samples of your work, until you find one willing to work for you. Agents, especially successful ones, would rather represent only known and successful clients, but being professionals, they are able to recognize a good idea, and you should at least get a fair appraisal of your work.

OTHER PROSPECTS

Sales of radio and television ideas are often made in strange and roundabout ways. If you have an idea for a program that would work best or be more salable if a particular actor or actress were involved with it, write to the person or his talent agent telling (in a general way) of the idea. A complete alphabetical listing of actors, actresses, singers, announcers, directors, choreographers, and stage managers is available in *Players Guide*, 165 West 46th Street, New York, New York 10036. Check your library.

THE SHOTGUN TECHNIQUE

One very important feature of selling broadcast ideas is that you can send them to more than one potential buyer at the same time. In the publishing industry it is a long established practice to send your books or magazine articles to one publisher at a time; you wait (sometimes months) for an answer before you can send it to someone else. But in radio and television it is well within custom and quite ethical to duplicate your work, by mimeograph, carbon copies, or other means, and send it simultaneously to as many prospects as you can find. However, check Chapters 7, 8, and 9 before you do this.

Selling Inventions and New Product Ideas

Whether called the invention industry or research and development, more than one million people are involved in creating and developing new ideas for a market that will spend billions of dollars on them. You might think that a million people actively working at the business of inventing would have long ago thought of everything possible and worthy of inventing. That is not the case. The number of inventions and patents increase every year. The U.S. Patent Office grants a new patent every few minutes. In addition, there are many inventions and new products sold for which no patent was ever issued.

The field of inventions is a broad one, covering many areas. Inventions may be industrial, consumer, or military and can involve mechanical products, electronic devices, methods or processes, chemical formulas, medical equipment and medicine, assemblies, improved construction or operation, innovations, containers and packaging, control devices, power and fuel systems, designs, prefabrication—almost anything you can point a finger at is someone's invention. This includes toys, games, novelties, cosmetics—even new plants and plant seedlings.

At what point in the development and protection of your idea should you try to sell it? There is no right answer to this question; you have a number of choices. You may sell your idea for an invention as soon as you have it and are able to describe it properly. It isn't necessary that an invention be patented before it can be offered for sale; in fact, some manufacturers would prefer that it was not patented, because they would rather handle the patenting themselves or perhaps elect (when possible) not to patent the idea at all and keep it a company secret.

Other manufacturers will consider the purchase of an unpatented invention but will want to know if it meets the requirements of the U.S. Patent Office for patenting—that is, the invention must be *new* and have *utility*. Your own judgment will tell you if your invention has utility—if it is useful to someone. The question of newness will probably require a search of patents previously issued. You can conduct this search yourself or hire a professional researcher or patent attorney.

Still other manufacturers will consider only those inventions for which a patent has been issued or for which a patent application has been made and is pending. If you wish to follow this procedure, it is strongly recommended that you retain the services of a patent attorney to lead you through the intricacies of preparing a patent application.

Regardless of the course you choose to take in selling your invention, there is one thing you must do before you do anything else. As soon as possible, prepare a *disclosure* of your idea. This is an inclusive written record describing your invention and a sketch, in as much detail as necessary, of its operation. Show this to two or more close friends or relatives to make sure that your description and sketch are explicit and understandable, and then ask them to witness your disclosure by signing and dating it. This may someday prove valuable as evidence that you were the originator of the invention.

Various versions of disclosure forms can be obtained from patent and invention brokers without charge or obligation on your part. Although you can reach these brokers through their advertisements in the classified sections of magazines such as *Popular Science* and *Science & Mechanics* or through the yellow pages, your lawyer or patent attorney can best advise you in this area.

Patent and invention brokers are often successfully used by inventors. They are professionals in the business of bringing inventor and manufacturer together; they have valuable contacts and mailing lists of buyers. Their experience in this type of selling and in the contacts involved can be very desirable.

There are two basic contracts into which you can enter with most brokers of this kind. The first is one where your payment to the broker is dependent on his sale of your invention. His commission is based on a percentage of the sale, whether an outright lump sum payment, licensing, or royalty agreement.

Other brokers will require an advance fee for their

time spent in attempting to sell your invention. They may or may not also require additional payment in the form of a commission based on the sale price. Some will reduce their commission payment on a sale by the amount of the advance fee. Select a broker with care; find one with an established reputation and with sales to his credit. You must realize that it is possible for an unscrupulous broker to earn a living collecting advance fees and never making a sale.

For reasons of your own, you may decide not to use a broker, but instead elect to reach manufacturers directly. In this case there are three things you must remember:

1. Make sure that your invention is compatible with the prospective manufacturer's own business. Check the sources provided in this book, and make certain you don't propose to sell an invention for an air-conditioning system to a company that makes paper novelties.

2. Whether or not you have a patent, you will save yourself time and trouble if you first write to a manufacturer giving him the general nature of your invention before revealing its actual operation. Not only will this enable you to determine if he has any interest in your idea, but he may also provide you with his company's release form or a statement of conditions under which he would consider your invention. This is extremely important if you are not protected by a patent.

3. Assuming that you have interested someone in looking at your idea, you must present it in a way that will help insure its sale. The basic information

you've committed to paper in your disclosure or patent application is not enough. Although the businessmen you will be addressing will make their decision to buy or not to buy on sound and rational economic factors, they are still human beings susceptible to time-proven selling techniques. In other words, sell your invention as you would sell anything else.

In addition to the basic description, give your invention a consumer-oriented name; stress the consumer benefits and its sale possibilities; emphasize its newness, its distinctive and unique features; mention its profitability to the manufacturer and the ease of production. Don't be overly enthusiastic or make claims that aren't true, or you might be regarded as an amateur and hurt your chances for the sale.

If you have been issued a patent, you can have it listed in the *Official Gazette of the Patent Office* at a small cost. This publication will reach potential buyers. Write to the U.S. Patent Office in Washington, D.C., for sample copies and more information. Check Chapter 3 for sources of prospective buyers. Chapter 12 has sample letters and release forms which can be of value to you.

Selling
All Other
Ideas

The advertising business, the invention business, and the broadcasting business are all businesses of ideas—built upon and kept alive by ideas. Ideas are offered for sale to and bought by these industries every day of the year. But the world of ideas is not limited to these fields alone.

This book attempts to cover the most prevalent and familiar areas where ideas can most easily be sold. One of the reasons why these areas have been selected is because custom and tradition have established idea-selling systems whereby buyers and sellers can come together with one understanding the other. There are areas not yet mentioned where the sale of ideas is common practice. This chapter covers a number of them.

Books

Your idea for a book can take many forms. Many publishers prefer that you first submit a brief description of the book you plan in order to determine interest in the idea. Other publishers will ask you to send along a complete outline of the book and a few sample chapters. Few, if any, publishers will refuse to look at your work if you send a complete manuscript.

The subject of the book can be anything legal. The two basic categories and some of the popular topics are:

1. Fiction: general adult, adolescent, children's, humor, tragedy, classic reprints, translations, romance, war, western, science fiction, fantasy, crime, mystery, satire, historical.

2. Nonfiction: travel, business, cooking, government, homecraft, social concern, marriage, human relations, family, sex, biography, autobiography, Americana, school texts, poetry, religion, self-improvement, photography, inspirational, history, education, leadership, instructional, philosophy, the arts, sports, cartoons, crossword puzzles, almanacs, health.

More information about book publishers and how to reach them can be found in *Literary Market Place,* at your library or bookstore.

Short Stories and Articles

Short stories and articles are the magazine equivalents of the book topics discussed above, and you may find them easier to produce and sell than complete books. The more ideas you can produce, the greater your chances of selling.

Millions of words have been written advising authors and would-be authors on how to sell their writings. Style, point of view, and treatment are all important, but if you are interested in selling as much as possible in the least amount of time, there are two *musts:*

1. Study your markets. Check the magazines to see what type of writing they usually feature.

2. Make sure that what you send them is suitable, new, and completely original. Your sources: *Literary Market Place* and the many "writer's" magazines found at your newsstand.

Photographs, Poetry, Cartoons, Jokes

Magazines are your best prospects for photographs, poetry, cartoons, and jokes. Publishers will also consider these as topics for a book, and there are many newspapers that will buy photographs and cartoons. Cartoon ideas can be developed into cartoon strips and syndicated to the newspapers throughout the country on a regular basis. Newspaper syndicates are also interested in ideas for regular newspaper columns. *Literary Market Place, Standard Rate and Data (Newspapers),* and the sources mentioned in Chapter 3 will help you reach these markets.

Stage and Screen Plays

Stage and screen plays are high-risk áreas. In both the motion-picture business and the legitimate theater the dollar investment is always great, and the possibility of a severe loss is always present. This is one of the reasons why producers would rather not take time nor risk temptation in reading unsolicited manuscripts, especially from unknown writers. Nothing can prevent you from writing to these people, but you'll fare much better in the long run if you first try to interest an agent in your work.

A Word about Agents

There are many agents for every literary and talent category mentioned in this book. As in every business some are better and more successful than others. Finding an agent to sell your work and advise you effectively is a hit-or-miss proposition. If you are an established writer, you can literally pick and choose until you find one who can satisfy you. If you have yet to make a sale, what you must do is bundle up the work you have ready and send it to an agent. If he shows no interest and returns it, send it to another agent. Keep this up until you find one. Few agents cover all areas of literary or artistic endeavor. They tend to specialize in certain types of work or fields. Check the yellow pages of major city directories as well as *Literary Market Place*.

Songs and Music

Here again, there is more than one way to go about selling your ideas. You can simply put words and music on paper and mail it off to song publishers, recording companies, performing artists, or agents who handle this type of work. Your source is the *Billboard '75 International Directory*. Also check the American Society of Composers, Authors and Publishers (ASCAP) at 575 Madison Avenue, New York, New York 10022.

Because many people today who are able to write music and lyrics also have a knowledge of musical instruments and are able to perform, the trend in selling this type of work has been toward demonstration. Music and lyrics are usually sold together, very often because of a performance, "live" at the prospective buyer's place of business or through a "demo-tape" recording sent through the mail. More and more often today, the performing talent is offered for sale along with his compositions, and it will sometimes happen that a buyer will not be interested in the songs but will want to sign the performer to a contract.

Business Plans, Systems, and Ideas

Every so often you will read about an employee who put an idea in his company's suggestion box and suddenly found himself a rich and famous man. If your own employer has established some sort of compensation or recognition system to reward ideas, you should try to sell him your idea. (If he has no such system, you might give him the idea of starting one.) Some employers will not consider the purchase of ideas from their employees; they expect to get them for nothing, as part of the terms of employment. If you are in such a situation, you have a moral obligation to respect the conditions of your employment.

If your idea is not connected with the business you are in and can be used only in some other business, you should ordinarily be able to sell where you wish. Of course, if you are unemployed, you may sell your idea anywhere.

Ideas encompass everything in the world. This includes every place of business in the world. Your business ideas can fall into one or more categories. Use the list below to broaden your application of your ideas and to develop new ones.

Inventory: physical location, control, reordering, etc.

Shipping: automatic, rates, scheduling, transportation, etc.

Personnel: hiring-firing, practices, unions, safety, etc.

Production: new processes, methods, cost-cutting, etc.

Purchasing: new sources, purchase orders, procedures, etc.

Accounting: new systems, electronic data processing, etc.

Retailing: self-service, credit, location of merchandise, etc.

Management: training programs, chain of command, promotion, etc.

Research and development: idea sources, consulting firms, etc.

Customer relations: returns policy, complaint handling, etc.

Selling: salesmen's aids, discounts, deals, premiums, etc.

These are but a few examples of the idea categories that come under the heading of "Business." In its broadest definition marketing means everything that takes place from the time of the original idea until the time when the product or service is consumed or utilized by the consumer. And along the way are countless opportunities for the application of new ideas.

Publicity Ideas

We are all familiar with the object of publicity: to bring information before the public at little or no cost. Many big businesses and important individuals employ the services of publicists, press agents, and public-relations experts. Businesses are concerned with maintaining a favorable public image (and will sometimes use paid advertising space to do this) or may wish to obtain free editorial space to announce new products or give news about their employees. Individuals, such as actors, use publicity to attract attention to themselves and enhance their fame.

It is very possible that you could interest someone in your idea to generate publicity. You could contact publicity agents or businesses and individuals directly. The Public Relations Society of America, 845 Third Avenue, New York, New York 10022, has a directory of members which is available at most libraries.

Fashion Design

Fashion design is not restricted to the beautiful gowns in glamour magazines. It includes the design of all wearing apparel and accessories for infants, children, and adults of both sexes, such as dresses, shirts, suits, sportswear, blouses, skirts, shoes, stockings, belts, undergarments, sleepwear, jewelry, handbags, neckties, gloves, hats, boots, and many other items. Although you may wish to sell individual design ideas to manufacturers (check Chapter 3), you might have better success in selling your talent by showing samples of your work to employers.

Other Ideas

The preceding information has been broad enough in scope to cover most of the important idea areas where it is possible for you to make money. With the information you have obtained you should have no difficulty in coping with the few remaining areas not covered specifically in this book.

Remember the importance of persistence. There has always been a shortage of ideas in this world, and there have always been thousands upon thousands of potential buyers. The trick is, and always has been, to locate the interested buyer at the right time.

Protecting Your Ideas by Copyright

7

A copyright protects the literary or artistic expression and form of your ideas but does not protect the idea, or concept, itself. In many instances, such as books or play scripts, the idea is interwoven inextricably with the manner of its expression and is therefore given some measure of protection. In addition to the formal protection afforded by the United States Copyright Office, there is also common-law protection.

In the United States literary property in an author's unpublished work is automatically protected from the moment of its creation by virtue of the so-called common law. This form of protection for an unpublished work is perpetual, so long as it remains unpublished, unless the author either releases his work to the public or secures a statutory copyright.

Authorized general publication of an author's work constitutes an abandonment of his common-law rights. Such a general and unrestricted release of his creation is considered a dedication to the public use, and his common-law rights are thereby destroyed. The work then goes into the public domain unless statutory copyright is obtained. An author may assign his common-law rights, thus permitting the assignee to claim statutory copyright as proprietor of the work.

Statutory Copyright

A statutory copyright is obtained by compliance with the provisions of the copyright law. There are a number of rights embraced in a statutory copyright, preserving for authors, composers, and artists the exclusive right to their writing for a limited time for the purpose of promoting the progress of science and the useful arts.

The law generally grants to the proprietor of the copyright the exclusive right to print, reprint, publish, copy and sell, translate, dramatize, arrange, and so forth the copyrighted work. The law also grants other rights, subject to certain limitations, such as the right to control the public performance of a work and to make recordings of it. These other rights vary with the nature of the work.

Only an author or those deriving their rights through him can rightfully claim copyright. There is no provision for securing a blanket copyright to cover all works of an author. Each work must be copyrighted separately if protection is desired. In the case of works made for hire it is the employer who is entitled to the copyright and not the employee.

What May Be Copyrighted

The Copyright Law (Title 17, United States Code) lists thirteen broad classes of works in which copyright may be claimed, with the provision that these are not to be held to limit the subject matter of copyright. The classes named and the materials cited as pertinent to each under the regulations are:

Books (Class A): works of fiction and nonfiction, poems, compilations, composite works, directories, catalogs, annual publications, information in tabular form, and similar text matter, with or without illustrations, published as a book, pamphlet, leaflet, card, single page, or the like.

Periodicals (Class B): such publications as newspapers, magazines, reviews, bulletins, and serial publications, which appear at intervals of less than a year; also contributions to periodicals.

Lectures or similar productions prepared for oral delivery (Class C): unpublished works such as lectures, sermons, addresses, monologues, recording scripts, and certain forms of television and radio scripts.

Dramatic and nondramatic musical compositions (Class D): dramatic works such as plays, scripts (for radio or television broadcast), pantomimes, ballets, musical comedies, and operas.

Musical compositions (Class E): all musical compositions (other than dramatic-musical) with or without words, as well as new versions of musical compositions, such as adaptations, arrangements, and editing when such editing is the writing of an author.

Maps (Class F): all published terrestrial maps and atlases, marine charts, celestial maps, and such three-dimensional works as globes and relief models.

Works of art; models or designs for works of art (Class G): works of artistic craftsmanship, insofar as their form but not their mechanical or utilitarian aspects are concerned, such as artistic jewelry, enamels, glasswear, and tapestries, as well as all works belonging to the fine arts, such as paintings, drawings, and sculpture.

Reproductions of works of art (Class H): published reproductions of existing works of art in the same or a different medium, such as a lithograph, photoengraving, etching, or drawing of a painting, sculpture, or other work of art.

Drawings or plastic works of a scientific or technical character (Class I): diagrams or models illustrating scientific or technical works or formulating scientific or technical information in linear or plastic form, such as an architect's or an egnineer's plan or design, a mechanical drawing, or an anatomical model.

Photographs (Class J): photographic prints and film strips, slide films, and industrial slides. Photoengravings and other photomechanical reproductions of photographs are registered in Class K.

Prints, pictorial illustrations, and commercial prints and labels (Class K): prints or pictorial illustrations, greeting cards, picture postcards, and similar prints, produced by means of lithography, photoengraving, or other means of reproduction. A print or label, not a trademark, published in connection with the sale or advertisement of an article of merchandise is also registered in this class.

Motion-picture photoplays (Class L): motion pictures, dramatic in character, such as features, serials, animated cartoons, musical plays, and similar productions intended for projection on a screen or for transmission by television or other means.

Motion pictures other than photoplays (Class M): nondramatic motion pictures, such as newsreels, musical shorts, travelogues, educational and vocational guidance films, and similar productions intended for projection on a screen or for transmission by television or other means.

Material That Cannot Be Copyrighted

The fact that a work does not fit conveniently into one of the thirteen classes does not necessarily mean that it may not be copyrighted. However, there are several categories of material that do not appear to be eligible for statutory copyright protection. These include, among others:

1. Words and short phrases such as names, titles, and slogans; familar symbols or designs; mere variations of typographic ornamentation, lettering, or coloring; mere listing of ingredients or contents.

2. Works designed for recording information which do not in themselves convey information,

such as time cards, graph paper, account books, diaries, and the like.

3. Work consisting entirely of information that is common property pertaining to original authorship, such as standard calendars, height and weight charts, tape measures and rulers, schedules of sporting events, and lists or tables taken from public documents or other common sources.

4. Sound recordings and the performances recorded on them.

How to Secure a Copyright

In order to secure and maintain statutory copyright protection in a published work, it is essential that all published copies contain a *copyright notice*. This should consist of three elements: (a) the word "Copyright," the abbreviation "Copr.," or the letter "c" enclosed in a circle; (b) the name of the copyright owner; (c) the year date of publication. These three elements should appear together on the copies; for example, "Copyright John Doe 1972." It is the act of publication with notice that secures copyright protection in a published work; the Copyright Office registers claims but does not grant copyrights.

If a work is published without the required copyright notice, copyright protection is lost permanently, and the work enters the public domain. Even adding the notice to later copies would not restore protection or permit the Copyright Office to register a claim.

Statutory copyright in unpublished works is secured by registering a claim in the Copyright Office. For this purpose it is necessary to forward an application form and a copy of the material to be copyrighted.

The appropriate form may be ordered from the Copyright Office. Use the listing above as a guide. *Note:* Forms A, B, F, H, and K may not be used for unpublished works.

In the case of manuscripts one complete copy should accompany the application. It will be retained by the Copyright Office. Special requirements concerning motion pictures, photographs, and certain graphic and artistic works are stated on the application forms.

Three steps should be taken in order to secure and maintain statutory copyright in a published work:

1. Produce copies with copyright notice. First produce the work in copies by printing or other means of reproduction. It is essential that the copies bear a copyright notice in the required form.

2. Publish the work.

3. Register your claim in the Copyright Office. Promptly after publication, you should forward the application form, the required number of copies, and the fee.

A copyright may be transferred or assigned by an instrument in writing signed by the owner. The law also provides for the recording of assignments of copyright in the Copyright Office. The original signed instrument should be submitted for the purpose of recording. It will be returned following recording. To protect effectively an assignment executed in the United States, it should be recorded within three months from the date of execution.

Mail and other communications should be addressed to the Register of Copyrights, Library of Congress, Washington, D.C. 20540. Do not send cash; use money order or bank draft payable to the Register of Copyrights. Send all material in the same package: application, fee, and copies.

Copyright protection is valid for a period of twenty-eight years and is renewable for a second period of twenty-eight years.

Protecting
Your Ideas
by Patent

The expanding volume of patent grants since the Patent Office was established parallels our technical and industrial progress. In the period 1790–1799, only 268 patents were issued. Today they are granted at a rate exceeding 750 a week.

Despite this great volume of patent activity, many businessmen and inventors are still largely unfamiliar with patent protection and patenting procedures. Understanding the relationship between the businessman, the inventor, and the Patent Office can be very important.

Patents are exclusive property rights to an invention and are issued by the Commissioner of Patents, U.S. Department of Commerce. They give an inventor the right to exclude others from making, using, or selling his invention for a period of seventeen years in the United States and its territories and possessions. Patents cannot be renewed except

by an act of Congress. Design patents for nonfunctional, ornamental devices are granted for three and
a half, seven, or fourteen years, as the applicant
elects.

Trademarks are also issued by the Commissioner
of Patents to individuals or companies who distinguish, by name or symbol, a product used in commerce subject to regulation by Congress. A "trademark," as defined in the Trademark Act of 1946,
"includes any work, name, symbol, or device, or
any combination thereof adopted and used by a
manufacturer or merchant to identify his goods and
distinguish them from those manufactured or sold
by others." The primary function of a trademark is
to indicate origin. However, trademarks also serve
to guarantee the quality of the goods bearing the
mark and, through advertising, serve to create and
maintain a demand for the product.

Rights in a trademark are acquired only by use,
and the use must ordinarily continue if the rights
so acquired are to be preserved. Registration of a
trademark in the Patent Office does not in itself
create or establish any exclusive rights but is recognition by the government of the right of the owner
to use the mark in commerce to distinguish his goods
from those of others. In order to be eligible for
registration, a mark must be in use in commerce
which may lawfully be regulated by Congress—for
example, interstate commerce—at the time the application is filed. Registrations issued remain in force
for twenty years and may be renewed for a like
period.

Once you get an idea for a product or process

which you think original or patentable and superior to those already on the market, you should try to crystallize it in your mind. Once jelled, the idea should be put in writing in such a way as to provide legal evidence of origin, should this question arise at some later date. Next, you will probably need help in determining whether the device is novel and if so, in making proper application for a patent.

Professional assistance is strongly recommended, because patent procedures can be complicated. In addition, you may not know how to make use of all the technical advantages possible. For instance, you may not claim broad enough protection for your idea. Hence, as a rule, it is best to have your application filed by a patent lawyer or agent.

Establishing novelty is one of the most crucial and difficult determinations to make, involving two things: (1) analyzing the device according to the standards listed below and (2) seeing whether anyone else has patented it first.

Analyzing your device should be done according to the following standards of what is *patentable:*

1. Any *new* and *useful* process (primarily industrial or technical); machine; manufacture or composition of matter (generally chemical compounds, formulas, and the like); or any new and useful improvement thereof.

2. Any *new, original,* and ornamental *design* for an article of manufacture (nonoperating, nonfunctional device, such as a new auto body design). Note that a design patent may not always turn out to be valuable because commercially similar design can easily be made without infringing the patent.

3. Any *distinct* and *new* variety of plant, other than tuber-propagated, which is asexually reproduced.

Another way of analyzing your idea is to consider it in relation to what is *not patentable:*

1. An idea of itself (as opposed to a mechanical device).

2. A method of doing business, such as the assembly-line system; however, any structural or mechanical innovations employed might constitute patentable subject matter.

3. Printed matter (covered by copyright law).

4. An inoperable device.

5. An improvement in a device which is a result of mere mechanical skill (a new assembly of old parts or an adaptation of an old principle; aluminum window frames instead of the conventional wood) unless it is a new and novel approach.

Applications for patents on machines or processes for producing fissionable material can be filed with the Patent Office. In most instances, however, such applications, if allowed, might be withheld from issue if the subject matter affects national security and should not be made public.

The invention should also be tested for novelty by the following criteria:

1. Whether known or used by others in this country before the invention by the applicant.

2. Whether patented or described in a printed publication in this or a foreign country before the invention by the applicant.

3. Whether described in a printed publication more than one year prior to the date of application for patent in the United States.

4. Whether in public use or on sale in this country more than one year prior to the date of application for patent in the United States.

These points are important. For example, if you describe a new device in a printed publication or use it publicly or place it on sale, you must apply for a patent before one year has gone by; otherwise you lose any right to a patent.

Although marking your product "patent pending" after you have applied has no legal protective effect, it often tends to ward off potential infringers.

Patent Search

It is not necessary for you or your attorney to travel to Washington, D.C., to search Patent Office files. Arrangements may be made with associates in Washington to have this done. Only the files of patents granted are open to the public. Pending applications are kept in strictest secrecy, and no access is given to them except on written authority of the applicants or their duly authorized representatives. A search of patents, besides indicating whether your device is patentable, may also prove informative. It may disclose patents superior to your device but not already in production which might profitably be manufactured and sold by your company, or a valuable business association may result.

Caution

A patent by no means guarantees immunity to lawsuits; in fact, it sometimes seems to attract challenges as to its legality. As one patent lawyer has said, "A patent is merely a fighting interest in a lawsuit."

One of these snags is *interference*, when two or more applicants have pending applications for substantially the same invention. Since a patent can be granted to only one applicant, the parties in such a case must give proof of the date the invention was made. If no such evidence is available, the date of filing the application is used to settle the controversy.

Unauthorized manufacture, use, or sale of patented property constitutes *infringement*. The patent-owner may file suit in a federal court for damages and/or an injunction prohibiting the continued use or manufacture of his patented article. If an item is not marked "patented," the holder of the patent may sue for damages, but no damages can be received covering the period before the infringer is so notified. Moreover, no recovery of damages is possible for any infringement occurring more than six years before the filing of the complaint. The responsibility of locating infringers lies completely with the inventor.

If you think your product will sell in a foreign country, you should apply for patent in that country to prevent infringement. Consult an attorney or agent for assistance.

Once you have obtained a patent, you have several choices of action. If you have the facilities or can obtain them, you can manufacture and sell the article; you can sell all or part of the patent; you can license or assign it to someone else. The trickiest operation of all is selling part interest in a patent. Remember that joint ownership holds many pitfalls unless restricted by a contract. A joint owner, no matter how small his interest, may use the patent as the original owner. He may make use of or sell the item for his own profit, without regard to any other owner; and he may also sell his interest in it.

This is what could happen. An inventor offers to sell his patent for $100,000. The prospective buyer, however, claiming this is too expensive, proposes to buy part interest, or $10,000 of it. Unless specifically restrained from doing so by contract, the part owner could go ahead and manufacture and sell the item as if he owned it 100 percent, without accounting to the original owner.

Even though your invention passes the expert, impartial judgment of a patent examiner as to novelty and workability, it still must be commercially acceptable if you are to make money from it.

Application for a Patent

If after a preliminary search you find that your idea can be patented, the next step is the preparation of an application to be filed with the Commissioner of Patents, Washington, D.C., to whom all subsequent correspondence should be addressed. The application must include:

1. A written document which comprises a peti-

tion, a specification (descriptions and claims), and an oath.

2. A drawing in those cases in which a drawing is possible.

3. The government filing fee. Check current cost.

If the Patent Office examiner refuses to grant a patent on the basis of claims requested, the application may be appealed to the Board of Appeals of the Patent Office.

Under special conditions an application may be given "special treatment"—that is, taken up for examination before its normal turn is reached.

Check Chapter 13 for additional sources and suggested reading on patents.

Protection without Copyright or Patent

There exists no law in the United States that gives absolute protection for ideas. The previous two chapters have, however, shown that some ideas can be translated into forms that afford a reasonable degree of protection—forms that can be copyrighted or patented.

Copyrights, because they deal primarily with the manner of literary expression, can protect a book, a magazine article, a play, and other similar works by virtue of their registry with the U.S. Copyright Office. They cannot protect an *idea* for a book, article, or play. William Shirer's copyright to *The Rise and Fall of the Third Reich* protects the contents insofar as *literary expression* is concerned; it does not in any way prevent someone else from writing *about* the rise and fall of the Third Reich. Many books were in fact written about the growth

and subsequent defeat of this infamous German
power long before Mr. Shirer published his book.

Patents, which are granted for *new* and *useful*
ideas, cannot usually protect business plans, systems,
ideas to improve business methods or streamline operations, improvements in the design or appearance
of items already patented, ideas to increase the
salability of a product by the substitution of superior
materials for inferior ones, and other ideas which fall
into this general area of consideration.

Ideas for improving various compositions, including formulas, by the mere addition of a new flavor-
ing, a new scent, or the like, may make it possible
to offer a superior product to the public and thereby
make money for both the originator of the idea and
the manufacturer. The important questions are:
How can the idea man promote these valuable
ideas? How can they be protected? What steps can
be taken to profit from them?

Luckily, the idea man has certain rights and also
has recourse to the law in the protection of his ideas
—not the protection provided by specific "idea legis-
lation," but by the long-standing law of contracts, the
growth of legal opinion, and established precedents.

As far back as the early English courts, it was held
that a man had title to his originations, but unless
protectable by established law, those ideas become
public property as soon as divulged. This old common law has been passed down to become part of
our present code. There is little, if any, actual statutory law governing the exchange of ideas, but a
large body of court decisions in this field has ac-

cumulated. Much can be learned from the more important cases.

The requirement that the possessor of an idea must be able to prove that it was actually original with him was brought out by the suit of Moore v. Ford Motor Company, 43F (2nd) 685. Moore had conceived a thrift purchase plan adapted for use in the sale of automobiles. He wrote to the Ford Motor Company that he would like an opportunity to submit the plan, which he believed would increase the sale of their automobiles. Ford replied:

> If you will kindly write us in detail regarding the plan which you have in mind for increasing the sale of Ford cars, understanding that in doing so there will be no obligation on our part, we will be very glad to give the matter our careful attention and advise you whether or not we would be interested in the plan.

Thereupon, Moore submitted his plan in a letter, concluding with the following paragraph:

> The above is a general idea of what I have in mind. I understand it is subject to amendments and eliminations, but if it is useable I would very much like to aid in perfecting it. However, as called for in your letter, I am writing you with the understanding that there is no obligation on your part.

The Ford Company subsequently returned Moore's letter, stating that it would not be interested in the proposition. At a later date, Ford put into effect a weekly purchase plan which became nationally known. That plan was similar to the one submitted by Moore except as to specific differences in detail.

Moore then brought suit, contending that his plan had been appropriated by Ford. In the trial Moore relied on his own evidence; namely, the correspondence between himself and the Ford Motor Company, plus the copy of the plan as presented to Ford, which the latter had returned, marked "not interested." Ford called in witnesses testifying that various Ford dealers throughout the country had already been using similar plans; that is, weekly payment schemes whereby terms of purchase could be made easier.

The court held that there was no piracy, because there were too many differences in detail between Moore's plan and the one put into effect by Ford. Furthermore, said the court, the basic idea appeared to have been used in Christmas-savings-club plans, which were known throughout the country prior to Moore's proposal. Because the inventor could not establish that he was the first and true originator nor prove definitely that the Ford Motor Company had appropriated or copied his idea, Moore did not have any ground on which the suit could be sustained.

The requirements for protecting an idea with a contract were brought out in the case of Bowen v. Yankee Network, Inc., 46 Fed. Sup. 63. Bowen contended that the William Wrigley, Jr., Company pirated his valuable and novel idea for a "radio presentation." Bowen had submitted the plan to Wrigley, which after some delay returned it as unacceptable. Wrigley later disclosed the idea to Yankee Network, Inc. Soon, a weekly radio presentation entitled "Spreading New England Fame," containing the features and ideas set forth in Bowen's proposal, was produced on the network.

In court it was brought out (1) that Bowen voluntarily submitted his idea to Wrigley, (2) that because of the voluntary submission, there was no breach of trust or contract, and (3) that there was no correspondence or other evidence to show that the disclosure of the idea to Wrigley had been done with the understanding that there was any limitation upon the use of it by the company. As a result, it was held by the court that Bowen could have protected his idea by contract but that he failed to do so when he voluntarily communicated it. Whatever interest he had in the idea therefore became public property.

From this case we learn: (1) An idea made public, either by word of mouth or in writing, immediately becomes common property, and unless the plan is revealed under contract or by confidential disclosure, anyone can make use of that property without infringing any rights; (2) the voluntary submission of an idea does not set up a contractual relationship between the originator and the other party; (3) because of the lack of contract, no action of any kind can be brought by the originator for breach of trust or contract; (4) ideas can be protected, provided the originator follows certain procedures governed by the law of contracts.

Another decision that emphasized the importance of drawing up a contract to protect an idea was rendered in the Equitable Life Insurance Company case, 132 N.Y. 265. In this suit it was held that without denying that there may be property rights in an idea, trade secret, or system, it is obvious that the originator himself must protect it from escape or disclosure. If the innovation cannot be sold, negotiated for, or used without a disclosure, it would seem proper that some contract, either express or implied, should guard or regulate the divulgence. Otherwise, the idea becomes the acquisition of whoever receives it.

The law of contracts applies in *all* such instances, but for it to be binding, there must be a definite "meeting of the minds" (that is, agreement among parties concerned). Ideas must be original and novel and the conception of the person submitting them, and they must be submitted in explicit form. Any ambiguity could easily result in nullification of a contract because a definite proposal had not been made.

Furthermore, the fact that a businessman consents to examine an idea does not mean that he has to buy it or put it into use. Therefore, your contracts or correspondence may have a proviso whereby the potential buyer does not obligate himself in any way by appraising the idea submitted. This, of course, does not free him from obligation in the event that he does make use of the idea submitted. In the *Moore v. Ford Motor Company* case, it was held that all danger of subsequent demands or obligations cannot be avoided by merely stating, "No obligation whatsoever."

Thus, an idea man who creates something worthwhile, even though no patent or copyright protection is available, may be able to cash in on his innovation. Legal decisions aid him if he follows the procedure by which many unpatentable ideas can be safely handled. When offering intellectual property, he must be able to prove that he is the first and true originator, and he must have the assurance of a contract that his disclosure will be treated confidentially. Once an idea leaves the mind of the originator, except under specific contractual arrangements, that idea becomes public property. This is important enough to bear repetition.

The idea man can:

1. Establish priority to an idea.

2. Protect his idea by complying with the law of contracts.

3. Safely deal with others so that they may examine his idea to find out if they want to buy it.

4. Sue for breach of contract following misappropriation of an idea submitted in confidence and under contract.

5. Lose title to his idea if it is released to a second person under any condition other than under obligation to review in confidence.

6. Rely on a businessman's request to review in confidence.

The idea man cannot:

1. Reveal the idea without protection of some sort and still retain exclusive control.

2. Recover damages for misappropriation of his idea unless he can prove that he is the first and true originator.

3. Recover damages if the idea or any of its details are submitted unsolicited.

4. Recover damages unless there is a violation of a definite "meeting of the minds" between him and the other party as to specific conditions of disclosure.

5. Recover damages unless there has been obvious copying or use of any or all of the submitted idea.

With this information, then, it is a simple matter to establish basic procedures which can be followed when submitting ideas.

Most books, magazine articles, television plays, and the like are not copyrighted by the authors before they are submitted to publishers and producers. One reason is that tradition and common practice have made this type of legal protection virtually unnecessary. There have been accusations and court actions involving plagiarism in this field, but these are rare and seldom justified.

Most publishers and producers, certainly the major ones, are honest businessmen. Those few that may not be honest realize the jeopardy to their business reputation if they were to steal someone else's work. Another reason is that many authors simply do not wish to expend the time and money necessary to copyright their work. For example, most books must actually be published before a copyright can be issued. A typewritten manuscript usually does not qualify as copyrightable material.

You may feel that your idea, whether in the form of a completed work, an outline, or a synopsis, is so distinctive and valuable that you are reluctant to reveal it to anyone without first obtaining some kind of protection. In this case you can use the protection offered by the law of contracts.

Either you can prepare an agreement form similar to the ones shown in Chapter 12, or you can contact your prospective buyer and request that he provide you with copies of his own form. Some firms receiving your version of an agreement form may disregard it and send along one of their own for you to sign.

The same comments apply to advertising ideas sent to agencies, advertisers, or suppliers to the trade.

Inventions can be sold in various stages of development, with or without a patent. If you attempt to sell an invention without patent protection, you should give yourself the protection afforded by a contract with your prospective buyer.

Warning! Regardless of the type of idea you have and are trying to sell, remember the importance of a contract which states *that your disclosure will be treated confidentially.* If you voluntarily submit your idea to a prospective buyer without assurance that it will be treated confidentially, the idea may be lost to you forever.

There are many companies willing to review your ideas, suggestions, inventions, or improvements. Some of these will ask you to sign and return an agreement form stating that "no confidential relationship will be recognized." This clause is not inserted in their forms to allow them to steal your ideas. These companies simply want to protect themselves against lawsuits initiated by unscrupulous idea men. Many companies have members on their staffs whose job it is to develop ideas. The idea you submit may be very similar to one that the company itself is developing or may even be identical to one that the company has temporarily put aside. Without the "no confidential relationship" clause, any subsequent execution of these ideas could place the companies in awkward and costly predicaments.

Nevertheless, you should make an effort to have a prospective buyer sign *your* version of a protective contract. If you are unsuccessful, then the decision of disclosing your idea can be made only by you.

In addition to these types of protection, there are other things you can do to help establish that *you* developed your ideas and *when* this took place. Your idea's date of origination could prove to be extremely important if someone else claims ownership of the same or similar idea. If you should ever be involved in a situation where someone else claims to have had the same idea as yours, either of you might decide to bring the other to court. In this event the following would strengthen your position.

1. *Disclosure* of the idea. Put the idea on paper as soon as possible, and date it. See Chapter 12 for typical disclosure form.

2. *Witnessing* of the idea by two or more trusted friends or relatives, who should also date their signatures.

3. *Record-keeping* of all notes, diaries, correspondence, evidence of research, experiments, and similar materials, dated when possible.

4. *Notarization* of your disclosure form. This is a preferred method of witnessing and is usually accepted in court without question.

5. *U.S. mail protection.* Place a copy of your idea

in an envelope, and send it by registered mail to yourself or your lawyer. Do not open the letter unless it should become necessary in court.

If you are in doubt about how the protection of your ideas relates to the information in this or any other chapter, you should seek legal assistance. If you have any difficulty in understanding anything having to do with legal matters, take no chances and make no second guesses. Find help from qualified sources. Your ideas are too valuable to risk losing.

Starting Your Own Business to Sell Your Ideas

Setting up a business in order to sell your ideas is not practical for all of the categories mentioned in this book. It is simply not possible for most individuals to start a television or radio station, a motion-picture company, a publishing firm, or other type of business necessary to implement many of the ideas noted earlier. Also, some of your ideas might be modifications or improvements of previously existing ideas belonging to and protected by someone else, or they might have application only to the products or services of extremely large businesses with which the individual could not hope to compete.

However, almost all large businesses had their small start at one time or another, and every one of them was initiated as a result of an idea. If your idea is sound, your business should succeed. You can begin in a small way, on a part-time basis in addition to your regular work, and if possible, you can operate from your home. Working alone is not an insurmountable obstacle. There are thousands of successful one-man advertising agencies, art and copy services, printing shops, management/financial/ marketing consultants, manufacturing and distributing businesses, and so on. Many inventors who decided to make and sell their products themselves, rather than sell out to someone else, started in a garage or basement.

You may feel that your idea is too big or important for a basement operation or that you must devote all of your time to it. If this is so, you must proceed with extra caution. After protecting your idea in the best ways possible, you will be contacting many other businesses in the course of establishing your own: bankers for financial assistance, suppliers for materials, lawyers, distributors and agents for selling, etc.

No one chapter in any book can provide you with all the information needed to start a business. Printed below is a list of check points which can do the next best thing. It can tell you whether or not you *should* start a business and what kind of preparation must be made for the business you have in mind.

Are You the Type?

1. Have you rated your personal traits such as leadership, organizing ability, perseverance, and physical energy?

2. Have you had friends or associates rate you on them?

3. Have you considered getting a partner whose strong points will compensate for your weak ones?

4. Have you had any actual business experience?

What Are Your Chances for Success?

5. Do you have special technical skills or artistic or literary talent?

6. Have you obtained some basic management experience working for someone else?

7. Have you analyzed the recent business trends in your field?

8. Have you looked at business conditions in the area where you plan to locate or market your idea?

9. What is the competitive situation in this field?

10. Have you determined what size business you plan to establish in terms of annual income?

11. How much capital will you need to launch your business and maintain it until income arrives?

12. Can you estimate how much time will elapse before income matches all expenses, including profits?

13. What net profit should you make; do you need?

14. Will net profit divided by the investment result in a rate of return which compares favorably with the rate you can obtain from other investment opportunities?

How Much Capital Will You Need?

15. What total income from sales or services can you reasonably expect the first six months? The first year? The second year?

16. What percentage of this income will be clear profit?

17. Have you anticipated all future expenses, including additional salaries for assistance if necessary?

18. How does this income compare with what you could earn working for someone else?

19. Are you willing to risk uncertain income for the next year? The following year?

20. What is your total investment in cash, pledges, loans, inventory?

21. Do you have other assets which you could sell or on which you could borrow money?

22. Is there another source from which you could borrow money?

23. Have you talked to a banker?

24. Is he favorably impressed with your plan?

25. Do you have a financial reserve for unexpected needs?

26. Do all these sources cover your estimate of the total capital you will need?

Should You Share Ownership with Others?

27. Do you lack needed technical or management skills which can be satisfactorily supplied by one or more partners?

28. Do you need the financial assistance of one or more partners?

29. Have you checked the features of each form of organization (individual proprietorship, partnership, corporation) to see which will best fit your situation?

Where Should You Locate?

30. Do you know how much space you will need?

31. Do you know what type of office or building you will need?

32. Do you know of any special features you require in lighting, heating, ventilating, air conditioning, or parking facilities?

33. Have you listed the equipment and/or tools you will need room for?

34. If the proposed location does not meet nearly all your requirements, is there a sound reason why you should not wait and continue seeking a more ideal location?

35. Have you checked the United States Census Bureau population figures?

Should You Buy a Going Business?

36. Have you considered the advantages and disadvantages of buying a going business?

37. Have you compared what it would take to equip and stock a new business with the price asked for the business you are considering?

38. Have you learned why the present owner wants to sell?

39. Have you checked the owner's claims about the business with reports from an independent accountant's analysis of the figures?

40. Have you checked with the company's suppliers to obtain their ideas of the value of the business?

41. Do they think well of the proposition?

42. Is the stock of merchandise a questionable buy? Would a large proportion of it have to be disposed of at a loss? Is any of it out of date or unsalable?

43. Are the physical facilities old or in poor condition and, hence, overvalued?

44. Are you sure the accounts receivable are worth the asking price?

45. Is the present company's goodwill fairly valued?

46. Are you prepared to assume the liabilities, and are the creditors agreeable?

47. Has your lawyer checked to see if the title is good and if there is any lien against the assets?

48. Are there any back taxes to pay?

49. Have the sales been temporarily increased by conditions that are not likely to continue?

Are You Qualified to Supervise Buying and Selling?

50. Have you estimated your total stock requirements?

51. Do you know in what quantities users buy your product or service?

52. Do you know how often?

53. Have you made a sales analysis to determine major lines to be carried?

54. Have you decided what characteristics you will require in your goods?

55. Have you set up a model stock assortment to follow in your buying?

56. Have you investigated whether it will be cheaper to buy large quantities infrequently or small quantities frequently?

57. What are the price differentials for large orders against capital and space tied up?

58. What merchandise will you buy direct from manufacturers and what from wholesalers?

59. Should your buying be restricted to a few suppliers?

60. Do you have control plans for buying and stocking?

How Will You Price Your Products and Services?

61. What prices, at varying sales levels, will you have to charge to cover expenses and make a profit?

62. How do these compare with competitive prices?

What Selling Methods Will You Use?

63. Have you studied the sales promotion methods customarily used in your line of business?

64. What will be your own policy?

65. Have you asked yourself why customers should buy your product—price, location, service, credit, quality, distinctive styling, uniqueness, others?

66. Will you do outside selling?

67. Will you advertise in newspapers?

68. Direct mail?

69. Posters and handbills?

70. Radio and television?

How Will You Manage Personnel?

71. Will you be able to hire satisfactory employees locally?

72. Do you know what skills and talents are necessary?

73. What are the prevailing wage scales and fringe benefits?

74. Can you afford that?

75. Have you considered hiring someone now employed by a competitor?

76. What are the pros and cons of doing this?

77. Do you plan training procedures?

What Records Will You Keep?

78. Have you a suitable bookkeeping system ready to operate?

79. Have you planned a merchandise control system?

80. Have you obtained the standard operating ratios for your type of business to use as a guide?

81. Have you provided for additional records as necessary?

82. Have you a system to use in keeping a check on costs?

83. Do you need any special forms?

84. Can you arrange to have all this done professionally?

What Laws Will Affect You?

85. Have you investigated what licenses to do business are necessary in your city, county, state?

86. Have you checked the health regulations?

87. Are your operations subject to interstate regulations?

88. Have you seen your lawyer for advice on how to meet your legal responsibilities?

What Other Problems Will You Face?

89. Have you worked out a system to handle your taxes?

90. Have you arranged for adequate insurance coverage?

91. Do you plan to build a management team?

92. Do your relatives and friends agree with your idea, and are they cooperative?

93. Can you carry accounts receivable with your capital?

94. What types of credit will you offer?

95. Will you have a definite returned-goods policy?

96. Have you considered what other management policies must be established?

97. Have you planned how you will organize and assign work?

98. Have you made a work plan for yourself?

99. How will you keep up with new developments in your line of business?

100. Where will you go for help in solving new problems that will arise?

If this short checklist has uncovered areas of information in which your knowledge could be increased, consult Chapter 13 for recommended sources and suggested reading.

Selling Your Ideas by Mail Order

The popularity of success stories about selling by mail has created the impression that selling by mail from one's home is a simple, easy method of substantially supplementing one's income in spare time. Success in mail selling calls for study, experience, some capital, organizing ability, and courage in meeting reverses. There are many pitfalls for the beginner.

A Part-time Beginning

Experience indicates it is wise for beginners in the mail-order business to start on a part-time basis and to operate from their homes. Another source of income, at least in the start, is considered essential. Expansion should be undertaken only after experience has demonstrated it to be advisable and feasible.

Who Buys by Mail and Why

A knowledge of why people buy through the mails is helpful. The mail-buying public can be grouped by buying motives into a number of classes, some of which are:

1. Those interested in novelties. They want something different from what their neighbors have. These people look over magazines for new ideas and items that might appeal to them.

2. Those pursuing a hobby or some particular line of interest, such as home gardeners, woodworking enthusiasts, etc.

3. Those who buy by mail as a matter of convenience. They find it easier to buy by mail especially if they live some distance from adequate shopping facilities.

4. Those who buy by mail purely for what they consider a price advantage.

The prospective mail dealer needs to determine whom he wishes to reach in his advertising and how well he can do the job of selling in the face of possible competition. Usually he cannot sell necessities and convenience goods supplied by local stores and shops at a price that will be low enough to attract business. To be successful, a mail offering should be unique or at least out of the ordinary.

Criteria for the Selection of Merchandise

There are no set rules that will guarantee a proper choice of merchandise, but there are a minimum number of requirements that each selection should meet.

1. Is it in competition with local stores or with well-known mail-order houses? You must be able to offer some buying advantages such as unusualness of the article, lower price, or wider selection of styles or models.

2. Do the goods have novelty or special appeal? Many mail enterprisers owe their success in part to the fact that their articles were not identical to what was available elsewhere. The items should be distinctive, easy to mail, and not easily broken. Seasonal goods, because of their short selling period, can prove hazardous for the small operator.

3. Do sales of the merchandise depend on sight appeal? Many kinds of goods are selected by customers because of color, style, or some other feature of appearance. The beginner in mail order would do well to leave such to local retail stores.

4. Will the merchandise sell at the necessary markup? The formula usually given for mail-order success is "one third for cost of the item to be sold, one third for selling expenses, and one third for profit." Others will advise you that the cost of the item should be closer to one fifth of the retail price.

5. Will the merchandise invite repeat sales? These additional sales can be for replacements of products that have been consumed or for related items in the form of one-time specialties that do not wear out. Do not think in terms of one sale only—the costs in such a venture are prohibitive. Encourage repeat orders from the mail customers you have found.

6. Are all items in the line chosen to appeal to the

same prospects? It is important to select related items with one kind of customer in mind. This has the advantage of increasing the potential amount of business for each item. Also, it permits the use of smaller and more selective lists of prospects.

Sources of Supply

The beginner must carefully consider the possible sources of the merchandise he wishes to sell. His success or failure may well depend upon the adequacy of these sources.

1. Goods made by the seller. Many articles successfully sold by mail are products made or produced wholly or partially by the seller or prepared to his order. The small operator should benefit by possessing a proposition distinctly his own, not in direct competition with identical offerings available elsewhere.

2. Purchased goods. Many manufacturers and wholesalers are reluctant to handle small accounts, since these are often unprofitable. Because of this, one should be certain before soliciting business that he has a firm commitment from the supplier as to delivery, price, and continued supply.

3. Goods of both kinds. Some mail-order concerns that have exclusive lines of merchandise that are self-made or made-to-order find it wise to add to them by buying from outside suppliers. This may be done in order to combine the offer of several products in one mailing piece. While spending his major effort in pushing his principal product, a dealer

may want to offer one or more related articles which he has purchased for resale or which he can order sent by the manufacturer directly to the customer.

Developing a Clientele

The usual method of building a clientele is by advertising an inexpensive item which is particularly novel or attractive in order to invite a maximum number of replies. The reader may be urged to place his order in direct response to the advertisement, or he can be invited to send for a descriptive circular or catalog.

These advertisements often have a symbol tied in with the name and date of the publication carrying the advertisement so that the effectiveness of the media employed can be measured. Analysis of responses affords data by means of which cost per inquiry and cost per order can be computed. This information makes it possible to do more selective advertising. The names and addresses of persons answering the advertisement are used in compiling future mailing lists for additional offerings. As subsequent mailings are made, corrections are necessary to keep the list up-to-date. A mailing list is built and revised on the basis of probability that it will be profitable.

Another method of locating prospects is by the purchase or rental of mailing lists. Lists can be obtained from companies or individuals engaged in the list business. Mailing lists should be carefully selected to cover groups of known buying habits—for instance, a list of new mothers, teachers, or car-owners who have bought something by mail. The fact that they are on such a list of past purchasers indicates that they are likely to be interested in other mail-order goods suited to their needs. A list of names copied from a telephone directory would ordinarily be of little value, because nothing is known of the interests of these people nor whether they have ever ordered anything by mail.

Rules and Regulations

You should acquaint yourself with the federal, state, and local laws and regulations that govern the conduct of the business:

1. *Licenses or permits.* Neither the federal government nor, as a rule, city and state governments require a license or permit to conduct a general business by mail. Since requirements vary in different states, it would be well to inquire of the State Tax Commission, the state Secretary of State, the city or county clerk, or other appropriate official as to what tax and license laws, regulations, or ordinances must be complied with. Some individuals wish to conduct their mail-order venture under their own names, whereas others prefer to adopt a "company" or an assumed name. If a firm name or any other title is employed other than the personal name, this fact should be recorded at the local post office. There is no charge for this service. If you plan to use a name other than your own, inquiry should be made of the local clerk of the court or county clerk to learn of

possible limitations imposed by the law. A company name can be registered at the city hall or local courthouse for a nominal charge. In some states a firm name must also be registered with the Secretary of State.

2. *Postal rules and regulations.* You should become familiar with the postal regulations that apply to your particular enterprise. The Post Office Department offers a variety of descriptive circulars, which are available without charge at local offices. If you are in doubt about anything relating to the use of the mails, the local postmaster or one of his aides will be glad to assist you. The beginner should become thoroughly acquainted with the classes and rates of the various postal services.

3. *Miscellaneous federal laws.* The mail dealer must be aware of federal regulations which might apply to his business. The Food and Drug Administration and the Internal Revenue Service can answer your questions in this regard. To the Federal Trade Commission is delegated the authority to prevent unfair methods of competition and unfair or deceptive acts or practices in interstate commerce. Correct labeling is essential, and restraint must be used to avoid exaggeration and the making of false claims.

4. *State sales and use taxes.* To what extent is the vendor of small mail-order specialty products responsible for the collection and payment of sales and use taxes imposed by those states into which he sends his goods? He has to pay state and city taxes (just as any other retailer) on items sold in the state or city in which he conducts his business. It is significant, however, that most states exempt casual

sales in interstate trade made through the mail. Where there is any question, dealers taking orders by mail from consumers for shipment of merchandise across state lines should get in touch with tax-collecting agencies of the states involved.

Adequate Records

Efficient record-keeping involves the preservation and recording of useful information in such a manner that analysis can be made from time to time. The following are suggested:

Financial files
Correspondence files
Prospect files
Customer records
Advertising records
Record of mailings
Inquiries to supply houses
Purchase record and inventory
"Things to do"

Materials Available

Much excellent literature is available if you wish to make a thorough study of mail-order methods. Chapter 13 has an extensive listing of information sources.

CHAPTER 1

Idea Checklist, Sample Letters, Forms and Contracts

It will be well worth your time to review the checklist below, keeping your ideas in mind, to make sure that you've covered all of the important points of consideration.

• Never lose your interest and enthusiasm in ideas. Everything sold today was first an idea.

• Study the first two chapters of this book until the idea-making process is second nature to you.

• Preparation will help ideas occur more easily, whether through conscious effort, subconsciously, or through accidental discovery.

• Be observant: Ask yourself how you could change and improve everything you see and hear.

• Keep a record of all the ideas that you have.

• Analyze and evaluate all of your ideas in light of today's market for them.

- Conduct research to learn of similar ideas that others may have had.
- Use the Idea Method in Chapter 2 to create more ideas and to develop the ones you have.
- Take your idea apart to see how many applications it could have.
- In describing your idea to a potential buyer, remember the basic techniques of salesmanship.
- Your idea description should have a "sizzle" and be exciting, but it should not be amateurish.
- Know your buyers. Check all potential sources.
- Don't waste time with "buyers" who aren't in a position to make a buying decision.
- Present your idea in a manner (format) with which the buyer you are contacting is familiar.
- Use every method you know to reach buyers: the mail, telephone, mutual contacts, personal interview, etc.
- Remember that in some fields you can use agents, brokers, and other representatives to help you sell your ideas.
- Protect your idea in every way possible: copyright, patent, contract, use of disclosure, witnesses, etc.
- Know your "idea category" intimately. Check the last chapter for information sources.
- Don't be limited to the topics discussed in this book—the world of ideas is much bigger.
- Consider establishing your own business, including mail order, to sell your ideas.
- Make sure you know your employer's policy regarding ideas before you attempt to sell them outside of your company.

• Don't delay. Do something about your ideas *now!*

In preparing to contact prospective buyers, the overriding considerations to remember are professionalism and sound judgment. Know all there is to know about your idea and what can be done with it. Be prepared to answer any questions. If possible, try to determine what your idea is worth—to you and to the buyers. Be realistic: Know your rights, and respect those of the company you are dealing with.

Sample Letters

It is always best to write first before attempting to reach anyone by telephone or in person. One reason is to determine if any interest exists in your idea (which will prevent you from wasting time), and another is to protect yourself by having correspondence records. Except for the few areas previously mentioned, never discuss your idea until you have protected yourself in some way.

If you are unsure as to which approach to use for a particular business, you may write a brief and simple letter like the following:

EXHIBIT A
First Letter

Your Address

Date

Inside Address

Gentlemen (or buyer's name):

I have an idea which is new and original with me and which could be of value to your business.

Please advise what procedure I should follow in submitting this idea to you.

Sincerely,

Your signature and name

Because some firms do not answer their correspondence immediately (and some not at all), you may decide to send many such letters to different companies at the same time. This will increase your chances for a favorable response in the least amount of time.

Some companies have adopted a policy of not considering ideas from sources outside of their business because they have been bothered by crackpots and amateurish troublemakers. Even these companies can be sold on looking at your idea if your approach is strong enough. You can achieve this by doing the following:

1. Mention your experience and familiarity with the field to which your idea is related.

2. Obtain professional references.

3. Write under a business or personal letterhead.

4. Allude to your idea without revealing it.

5. Make use of recognized trade and industrial terminology.

6. Note the profit potential.

EXHIBIT B
First Letter

(Letterhead)

Date

Inside address

Gentlemen (or buyer's name):

Applying the knowledge I've gained during my years with various paper-product companies, I have developed a new packaging idea which could greatly increase your profits through reduced processing and production costs. This idea would also heighten the salability of one of your present products. It involves a unique, inexpensive, and revolutionary method utilizing heat pressure and multiple die-cutting.

Enclosed is a statement from my employer allowing me to offer this idea to other companies. Also enclosed are letters of reference from previous employers. Please advise what procedure I should follow in submitting this idea for your consideration.

Sincerely,

Your signature and name

This same approach can be used for many of the idea categories mentioned in this book.

Another way to help convince prospective buyers of your professionalism is to include an Agreement to Review Idea with your letter. In this case you would substitute the last sentence of the Exhibit B letter with this paragraph:

EXHIBIT C

If you are interested in details of the idea, I shall be glad to forward complete information if you will kindly sign and return one copy of the enclosed agreement form.

EXHIBIT D
Agreement to Review Idea

We the undersigned agree to receive in confidence full details about an idea for product packaging [or other] to be submitted for our consideration by [your name].

It is further understood that we assume no responsibility whatever with respect to features which can be demonstrated to be already known to us. We also agree not to divulge any details of the idea submitted without permission of [your name] or to make use of any feature or information of which the said [your name] is the originator without payment of compensation to be fixed by negotiation with the said [your name] or his lawful representative.

It is specifically understood that in receiving the idea of [your name], the idea is being received and will be reviewed in confidence and that within a period of thirty days we will report to said [your name] the results of our findings and will advise whether or not we are interested in negotiating for the purchase of the right to use said idea.

Company _____

Street number _____

City _____ State _____ Zip code _____

Official to receive disclosures:

_____ Title _____

Date _____ Signature _____

Accepted [your name] _____

Signature _____

Of course, if your idea is protected by patent or copyright, you needn't be secretive in your first letter. You can reveal the basic idea and offer to send your prospect full details if there is any interest.

It was noted earlier that some publishers prefer that writers contact them prior to the submission of ideas. Some publishers are interested only in specific subjects, such as trade or technical material. You can find this out by writing first, and if there is any interest, you can follow up by submitting what the publisher prefers: outline, synopsis, sample chapters, or completed work.

If you prefer to have someone try to sell your idea for you, you must interest such a representative, such as literary agents, talent agents, patent or invention brokers. If you contact an invention broker, you will likely receive a form which can serve as a "record of invention," which may be similar to the Idea Disclosure Form below. (Allow sufficient space in the form for both verbal description and illustrations.)

EXHIBIT E
Idea Disclosure Form

Date

This is to certify that [your name] is the originator of the [type of idea] described below.

Description:

(A) Construction

(B) Operation

(C) Application

Illustrations:

(A) Sketches of the idea

(B) Detail of vital parts

(C) Photographs if available

(Number the parts illustrated, and use these numbers when referring to the parts in the written description.)

Witnessed by_____ Date_____
_____ Date_____

(Include your name and signature and the date.)

Witnesses must be able to understand the idea being disclosed before signing the form. This same general format can be used as an idea-disclosure form for your personal protection or as a means of presenting the idea to an interested buyer.

On the disclosure form or record-of-invention form provided by a broker will be an additional paragraph which you will be asked to sign. It authorizes the brokerage firm to act in your behalf in attempting to sell your idea. Usually the words "in strict confidence" will appear. Look for them—they are important for your protection. There may also be a space for you to enter the amount of money you will consider for the sale of your idea—either a lump sum or a royalty arrangement. Use extreme caution in this area. Don't give your idea away. If possible, leave this area open for later negotiation. Important: Reserve the right (in writing) to revoke your agreement with the brokerage firm at any time.

Release Forms

One major United States firm, in business for over sixty years, has a policy of considering all ideas, suggestions, improvements, and inventions submitted to them. Before doing this, however, the firm requires that you sign an agreement that gives the company maximum legal protection. It is perhaps one of the most sophisticated relase forms ever prepared. Stripped of introductory remarks and legal jargon, the points covered are as follows:

EXHIBIT F
Company Release Form

(A) The [name of] Company will review and consider any ideas, suggestions, improvements, or inventions, but only if voluntarily submitted by the originator.

(B) Although proper care will be exercised in the handling of all such unsolicited ideas, the company incurs no legal obligations to deal with the originator in confidence.

(C) No obligation will be assumed by the company or any of its personnel or agents until and unless a formal written contract is entered into between the company and the originator.

(D) In consideration of the company reviewing these submissions, the originator releases the company from any liability in connection with said ideas.

_____ Date _____

(Originator's signature)

As forbidding as some release forms appear, behind most of them stand reputable companies with a strong sense of ethics and fair play. The phrasing may seem to indicate that these companies are intent upon stealing your ideas right and left, but such instances are extremely rare. Of course, if you have a patent, you may sign such a form without any reservation.

Advertising agencies, advertisers, or businesses in related industries or professions may send you a form similar to the following:

EXHIBIT G
Advertising Release Form

I wish to present the attached idea, which is original with me, with the understanding that I am doing so voluntarily and not at your solicitation. Your written decision that the idea is not original will be accepted by me.

I am to receive no compensation for said idea unless your decision is that the idea is original and valuable to you. Should the idea prove useful to you and/or to your clients, compensation for exclusive use shall be fixed by you. I understand that misunderstanding of this agreement shall be submitted to [a trade or professional association] for arbitration and their decision shall be binding.

_____ Date _____

(Originator's signature)

Accepted by _____

This form, too, may seem restrictive, and some of the earlier comments on other forms apply. Even if you should decide to sign such a form, you do not have to accept the amount of compensation fixed by the prospective buyer. You can still negotiate, or you can refuse to sell the idea if you cannot obtain a satisfactory settlement.

EXHIBIT H
Broadcast Release Form

I am submitting for your consideration the enclosed material described as [title, if any, and brief description or synopsis]. This property is original with me, and I have the sole and legal power to transfer ownership and/or grant all rights to the material herein described.

You are not to use this material unless we first agree, by written contract, to the terms of compensation for the use of said material. This does not restrict, however, your use of material identical or similar to my submission (or portions of it) which is not original with me or which you may already own.

Any disagreement arising out of your use of material, without compensation, that I feel is original with me shall be submitted to [a trade or professional association] for arbitration, whose decision shall be binding.

_____ Date _____

(Originator's signature)

In addition to these sample letters and release forms, you might find it interesting to review the following examples of actual communications received by the author from companies who invite the submission of ideas.

SUBMISSION LETTER AGREEMENT

RCA Corporation
P. O. Box 432
Princeton, New Jersey 08540

Attention: Submitted Ideas Section

Gentlemen:

The undersigned has submitted or is submitting with this letter or is about to disclose or demonstrate some ideas and/or information which may prove useful in RCA's business, and requests that RCA consider them.

As an inducement to RCA to consider the ideas and/or information, as well as any additional matter which may hereafter be submitted in connection with or related to the ideas and/or information, all of which are hereinafter collectively referred to as the material, the undersigned agrees that the submission thereof and any consideration which may be given to it at his request by RCA, shall be in accordance with the following terms and conditions, which shall be effective as of the date of the first submission by the undersigned of any material:

(1) The undersigned hereby warrants that he has the right to disclose the material; that there are no outstanding agreements of any kind which are inconsistent herewith; and that the submission of the material was not solicited by RCA and/or any of its representatives.

(2) The material is submitted to RCA on a completely nonconfidential basis.

(3) RCA assumes no obligation of any kind with respect to the material except that it will examine the material and, in due course, inform the undersigned whether RCA has any interest therein.

(4) RCA is not obligated in any way to use any of the material. However, the use to be made by RCA of any of the material, and the amount of compensation, if any, to be paid for such use, are matters resting solely within the discretion of RCA.

(5) RCA is not obligated in any way to discuss or to give any reasons for its decisions respecting any submission.

(6) RCA assumes no obligation of any kind to compensate the undersigned for any costs or expenses incurred in connection with the submission of the material.

(7) RCA is under no obligation of any kind to return any material, and RCA has the right to make and retain a copy or copies of any material.

(8) RCA has the right to require that all material be submitted in or translated into English.

As used herein "RCA" includes any subsidiary of RCA and "the undersigned" includes principals, if any, of the undersigned.

Notwithstanding any of the above-noted terms and conditions, it is understood that no release or license is granted to RCA with respect to the infringement of any valid patent or patents which the undersigned now holds or hereafter acquires.

Very truly yours,

List of enclosures, if any

_____
Signature of Submitter

_____
_____
Date

_____
(Title and Company, or Principals, if any)

_____
Address

Pat. 3250 4/71

PER NOVELTY MANUFACTURING COMPANY

NRY STREET • STAMFORD, CONN. 06904 • 203-325-2671 • CABLE: 'DOUBLGLO' STAMFORD • CHRISTMAS   DECORATIONS   VALENTINE!

UBL*GLO

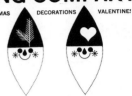

Dear Mr.

We sincerely appreciate the interest of persons outside our
organization who wish to submit ideas or inventions to us.
We realize that useful developments may originate from outside
sources and desire to give careful consideration to any new
and patentable ideas or inventions.

In order to avoid misunderstanding, and for your protection, as
well as our own, we have adopted the following procedure.

A description or disclosure of the idea or invention should be
submitted in writing. This procedure should be likewise followed
if further information is needed incidental to that previously
submitted.

An exact copy of the written description should be kept by the
person presenting it, since we retain in our files the material
submitted to us. Thus, both of us will have a record of the
exact data supplied, thereby removing the possibility for any
future misunderstanding as to just what was submitted.

This written information should be in the form of a copy of the
patent application filed in the Patent Office, with the filing
date and serial number omitted, or, if no patent application has
been filed, a complete written description, accompanied by
sketches or drawings of the idea or invention, and duly witnessed
by competent persons familiar with the discolsure. (In case a
patent has already been issued covering the idea or invention,
then this letter need not be signed. In such case we would like
a copy of the issued patent.)

As soon as reasonably possible, the disclosure will be referred
to such of our officials as are selected by us for its review.
At times, it may be desirable for us to consult outsiders about
the material submitted, in order to enable us to arrive at a
decision as to both its practicability and value to us.

For this reason, it is agreed that our acceptance and consideration
of the idea or invention submitted is upon the condition that
we will not be expected, or requested, to treat such disclosures
as secret or confidential, and that these disclosures do not
establish a confidential relationship of any kind. This provision
applies also to all additional disclosures made incidental to
the consideration of the original material submitted.

-2-

It frequently happens that similar ideas or inventions have been previously made by our own personnel, or are present in prior patents or patent applications owned by us, or by other persons. It is agreed that we are to be under no obligation to reveal the company's activities of the same or similar nature, or any such patent information, or the results of our investigation.

The rights arising out of the material submitted to us are to be measured and defined by the patent protection that may be given under the patent laws of the United States or under any valid patents issued upon such material, and we are to have all the rights that the public would have with respect to the idea or invention submitted.

The entering into negotiations for the purchase of any ideas or inventions submitted, or making of any offer for their purchase, shall not in any way prejudice us, nor shall this be deemed an admission of the novelty of the ideas of inventions, or of the priority or originality on the part of the person submitted or owning them.

Our Company will consider the ideas or inventions submitted only so far as in our judgment, they require consideration; and we assume no obligation, implied or expressed, more than to indicate in reply whether or not we are interested.

The foregoing conditions may not be modified except in writing agreed to by one of our duly authorized executives or officers.

If you agree to the above, please indicate your approval by dating and signing a copy of this memorandum.

PAPER NOVELTY MANUFACTURING COMPANY

By_____

ACCEPTED:

_____

Date: . . . .

Columbia Broadcasting System, Inc.
51 West 52nd Street
New York, New York 10019

Title of material
submitted: . . . .

. . . .

Gentlemen:

I am today submitting to you my above entitled material, which I have summarized on the attached page, upon the following understanding:

1. I represent that my material is original with me and that I have the exclusive right to grant all rights therein. Furthermore, I limit my claim of rights to the features of such material which are specifically described on the attached page. If my material is intended for use in connection with broadcasting or constitutes a program idea or format, I represent that my exclusive right to my material includes the exclusive right to license broadcasting rights therein. I claim exclusive rights in the title (if any) of my material only as regards its use in connection with my material.

2. You will not make any use of my material unless you shall first negotiate with me compensation for such use. I agree, however, that your use of material containing elements similar to or identical with those contained in my material shall not obligate you to negotiate with me nor entitle me to any compensation if, because such elements are not new or novel, or were not originated by me, or because other persons (including your employees) have submitted or prepared or may hereafter submit or prepare material containing similar or identical elements, or because of any other reason you determine that you have an independent legal right to use such material.

3. If you determine that you have the legal right to use material similar to or identical with mine, or containing elements similar to or identical with those contained in my material, without the payment of any compensation to me and proceed to use the same, and if I disagree with your determination (such disagreement to be indicated in writing to you no later than sixty (60) days after your first use of such material), I agree that if you so elect, the controversy between us shall be submitted to the New York Supreme Court for determination pursuant to the New York Simplified Procedure for Court Determination of Disputes.

4. I have retained a copy of my material, and you shall not be responsible for the preservation or return thereof.

Very truly yours,

. . . .

Name . . . .   (Print)

Name . . . .   (Signature)

Address . . . .

City . . . . State . . . .

Telephone No. . . . .

If under twenty-one (21) years of age signature of parent or guardian must be included below.

I represent that I am a parent (guardian) of the minor who has signed the above release and I agree that I and the said minor will be bound thereby. . . . .

Parent (Guardian)

POLICY CONCERNING SUBMISSION OF
IDEAS AND OTHER MATERIAL

We appreciate the courtesy of persons who suggest to us material such as ideas, broadcasting formats, literary material, merchandising schemes or plans, advertising slogans and other suggestions for our use. However, we receive many suggestions which have been made previously, either by our own staff or by others. Likewise we may at any time commence using material similar to yours which we received after the date of your submission. It has, therefore, become necessary for us to adopt the policy of refusing to consider any such material unless the person submitting it in person has signed the agreement below and has specified the maximum payment to be made to him in the event of our use of his material. KINDLY DO NOT SUBMIT TO US ANY MATERIAL WHICH YOU DEEM TO HAVE A VALUE IN EXCESS OF THE LIMITS SPECIFIED IN PARAGRAPH 1 OF THE BELOW AGREEMENT BETWEEN US. There are two copies of this agreement; please sign in the space provided and return one copy to us.

Warwick & Legler, Inc.
375 Park Avenue
New York 22, New York

Gentlemen:

In accordance with your above expressed policy concerning submission of ideas and other material, I am today submitting to you my material summarized on the reverse side pursuant to the following agreement:

1. You agree to cause your appropriate employee having the duty of evaluating material of the type now being submitted by me to review my material. I agree that you may use my material or one or more if its features or components. If you commence such use, and provided it is original, novel and valuable, you agree to pay me as total compensation therefor such sum of money as we may subsequently agree upon in writing. If we have not attempted or are unable to agree upon the amount of such payment and you use such material, you will pay and I will accept as full consideration for all rights of every kind, the sum of $250.00. I agree that I can suffer no damages in excess of the foregoing from your use of my material or for any other claim with respect thereto.

2. I declare that all of the important features of my material are summarized in the space provided and I have disclosed no other features to you. I warrant that the material is original with me and that no one else to my knowledge has any right to it. I believe my material and its features to be unique and novel. However, I recognize that other persons including your own employees may have submitted to you or to others, or made public, or may hereafter originate and submit, or make public, similar or identical material which you may have the right to use, and I understand that I will not be entitled to any compensation because of your use of such other similar or identical material.

3. Any controversy arising as to whether you used my material, or relating to this agreement, will be conclusively determined by arbitration as provided by New York Law and the rules and regulations of the American Arbitration Association. The decision of the arbitrator shall be controlled by the terms of this agreement and no award may exceed the amount specified in Paragraph 1. I agree that any action against you must be brought within six months after the date of your first use of my material, regardless of when my actual knowledge of said first use shall begin.

4. I have retained copy of my material submitted to you and release you from liability for loss or damage to such material.

5. This agreement constitutes our entire understanding. Any modification or waiver of its terms must be in writing, signed by both of us. The invalidity of any provisions hereof is not to affect the remaining provisions. This agreement applies equally to any other material which I may submit to you in the future or have in the past submitted to you unless agreed in writing to the contrary.

DATED:_____

NAME_____

AGREED:

ADDRESS_____

WARWICK & LEGLER, INC.

_____

By_____   _____
(Author or agent: Write on the back of this form a short summary of the contents of the material being submitted.)

Sources, Suggested Reading, Government Assistance

This chapter will provide you with the basic information you will need to locate additional information. Directories, encyclopedias, and guides; annual publications of selected industries and professions; books dealing with the major topics discussed previously; and government publications available at little or no cost are listed.

General Sources

Libraries are your best single source for any information. Not only can they help you locate any publication ever issued, but many of them also have telephone directories of the major cities in the United States, the yellow-page sections of which are important listings for anyone in the idea-selling business. Here are the major sources.

Davison's Textile Directory. Ridgewood, N.J.: Davison
Publishing Company, 1971.

Directory of Newspapers and Periodicals. Philadelphia:
N. W. Ayer & Son, Inc., 1970.

Dun & Bradstreet Million Dollar Directory. New York:
Dun & Bradstreet, 1972.

*Encyclopedia of Associations and National Organizations
of the United States.* Biannual. Detroit: Gale Research Company.

Guide to American Directories. Annual. Rye, N.Y.: B.
Klein Publications, Inc.

Hausdorfer, Walter. *Handbook of Commercial, Financial and Information Services.* New York: Special
Libraries Association, 1958.

Home Reference Books in Print. New York: R. R. Bowker
Company, 1970.

Jeweler's Buyers Guide. New York: Sherry Publishing
Company, 1971.

Juokins, J. C. *National Associations of the United States.*
Washington, D.C.: United States Department of
Commerce, 1949.

Kruzas, Anthony. *Directory of Special Libraries and Information Centers.* Detroit: Gale Research Company, 1968.

MacRae's Blue Book. Annual. Hinsdale, Ill.: MacRae's
Blue Book Company.

Manley, M. Catherine. *How to Find and Use It.* New
York: Harper & Row, Publishers, 1955.

Murphy, Robert. *How and Where to Look It Up.* New
York: McGraw-Hill Book Company, 1958.

Severn, William. *How to Turn Extra Time into Money.*
New York: Bartholemew House Ltd., 1958.

Trade Directories of the World. New York: Croner Publications, 1971.

In addition to the above, the Small Business Administration in Washington, D.C., makes available the following pamphlets: *Management and Technical Publications*

and *National Directories for Use in Marketing.* Standard Rate & Data Service, Inc., of Skokie, Illinois, publishes a number of rate and data books, available at your library, including *Business Publications* and *Consumer Publications.* These can give you information on any periodical published and help you to locate such specialized magazines as *Television Age, Direct Marketing,* and *Author and Journalist.* Listings are alphabetical.

Chapters 1 and 2

Cannon, W. B. "The Role of Chance in Discovery," *Scientific Monthly,* Vol. L (1940).

Haefele, John W. *Creativity and Innovation.* New York: Van Nostrand Reinhold Company, 1962.

Hutchinson, E. D. *How to Think Creatively.* Abington-Cokesbury, 1949.

Montmasson, J. M. *Invention and the Unconscious.* London: Kegan, Paul, Trench, Trubner, Publishers, 1931.

Osborn, Alexander. *Applied Imagination.* New York: Charles Scribner's Sons, 1953.

Wallas, G. *The Art of Thought.* New York: Harcourt Brace Jovanovich, Inc., 1926.

Young, James Webb. *A Technique for Producing Ideas.* New York: Advertising Publications, 1956.

Chapters 3, 4, 5, and 6

Advertising and Sales Promotion Buyers Guide. Annual. Chicago: Advertising Publications, Inc.

Advertising Specialty Register. Annual. Philadelphia: Advertising Specialty Institute.

Angerman, V. D. *How to Find a Buyer for Your Inven-*

tion. New York: Science & Mechanics Publishing, 1956.

Audio-Visual Marketplace. New York: R. R. Bowker Company, 1971.

Barton, Roger. *Advertising Agency Operations and Management.* New York: McGraw-Hill Book Company, 1955.

————. *Advertising Handbook.* Englewood Cliffs, N.J.: Prentice-Hall, Inc., 1950.

Beranger, Clara. *Writing for the Screen.* Dubuque, Iowa: W. C. Brown Company, Publishers, 1950.

Berry, Eric. *Writing for Children.* New York: The Viking Press, Inc., 1947.

Broadcasting Yearbook. Annual. 1735 De Sales Street, N.W., Washington, D.C.

Burton, Phillip, and Miller, J. Robert. *Advertising Fundamentals.* Scranton, Pa.: International Textbook, 1970.

Busfield, Roger M. *The Playwright's Art.* New York: Harper & Row, Publishers, 1958.

Editor and Publisher Market Guide. New York: Editor and Publisher, 1970.

Gehman, Richard. *How to Write and Sell Magazine Articles.* New York: Harper & Row, Publishers, 1959.

Graham, Irving. *Encyclopedia of Advertising.* New York: Fairchild Publications, 1952.

Greene, R. S. *Television Writing.* New York: Harper & Row, Publishers.

Groesbeck, Kenneth. *Advertising Agency Success.* New York: Harper & Row, Publishers, 1958.

Hailer, Arthur. *Close Up on Writing for Television.* Garden City, N.Y.: Doubleday & Company, Inc., 1960.

Higgins, Frank. *Inventing to Sell.* Arlington, Va.: Varsity Press, 1958.

How and Where to Get Free Publicity. Biannual. Kalamazoo, Mich.: Musselman Advertising.

International Reference Handbook of Marketing and

Advertising. Biannual. New York: World Trade Academy Press.

Keeley, Joseph. *Making Inventions Pay.* New York: McGraw-Hill Book Company, 1950.

Kerr, Walter. *How Not to Write a Play.* New York: Simon & Schuster, Inc., 1955.

Laughlin, Myron Penn. *Money from Ideas: A Primer on Inventions and Patents.* New York: Popular Mechanics Press, 1950.

Lesley, Philip. *Public Relations Handbook.* Englewood Cliffs, N.J.: Prentice-Hall, Inc., 1950.

Literary Market Place. New York: R. R. Bowker Company, 1971.

McHahan, Harry W. *The Television Handbook and Dictionary.* New York: Hastings House Publishers, Inc., 1957.

Madison Avenue Handbook. New York: Peter Glenn Publishers, 1971.

Meredith, Scott. *Writing to Sell.* New York: Harper & Row, Publishers, 1959.

Montgomery, Robert. *Television Writing—Theory and Technique.* Harper & Row, Publishers, 1956.

Moore, Arthur. *Invention, Discovery and Creativity.* Garden City, N.Y.: Doubleday & Company, Inc.

One Hundred Books on Advertising. Columbia, Mo.: University of Missouri School of Journalism, 1971.

Problems in Developing and Launching New Products. New York: American Management Association, 1952.

Reiss, Otto F. *How to Develop Profitable Ideas.* Englewood Cliffs, N.J.: Prentice-Hall, Inc., 1945.

Roberts, Edward B. *Television Writing and Selling.* Boston: The Writer, Inc., 1964.

Sandage, Charles, and Fryburger, Vernon. *Advertising Theory and Practice.* Homewood, Ill.: R. D. Irwin, Inc., 1971.

Schwab, Victor O. *How to Write a Good Advertisement.* New York: Harper & Row, Publishers, 1962.

Spring, Samuel. *Risks and Rights in Publishing: Tele-*

vision; Radio; Motion Pictures; Advertising and the Theater. New York: W. W. Norton & Company, Inc., 1952.

Standard Directory of Advertisers. Annual. Skokie, Ill.: National Register Publishing Co., Inc.

Standard Directory of Advertising Agencies. Annual. Skokie, Ill.: National Register Publishing Co., Inc.

Standard Rate and Data (Television and Radio). Skokie, Ill.: Standard Rate & Data Service, Inc., 1972.

Thomas Register of American Manufacturers. Annual. New York: Thomas Publishing Company.

Thompson, Joseph W. *Selling.* New York: McGraw-Hill Book Company, 1966.

Wainwright, Charles A. *Television Commercials.* New York: Hastings House Publishers, Inc., 1958.

————. *The Television Copywriter.* New York: Hastings House Publishers, Inc., 1958.

Weir, Walter. *On the Writing of Advertising.* New York: McGraw-Hill Book Company, 1960.

Yates, Raymond. *3100 Needed Inventions.* New York: Wilfred Funk, Inc., 1951.

Yoakem, Lola Goelet. *Television and Screen Writing.* Berkeley, Calif.: University of California Press, 1958.

In addition, the Small Business Administration in Washington, D.C., makes available the following pamphlets: *Products Listing Circular* and *New Product Development and Sale.* The U.S. Patent Office, Washington, D.C., offers the *Official Gazette of the Patent Office.*

Chapters 7, 8, and 9

Calvert, Robert. *Patent Practices and Invention Management.* New York: Reinhold Publishing Corporation, 1964.

Fenner, Terrence W. *Inventor's Handbook.* New York: Chemical Publishing Company, 1969.

Guide to Book Publishers. New York: R. R. Bowker Company, 1970.

Pilpet, Harriet F., and Goldberg, Morton David. *A Copyright Guide.* New York: R. R. Bowker Company (in cooperation with the Copyright Society of the U.S.A.), 1960.

Rhodes, Fred Hoffman. *Elements of Patent Laws.* New York: Cornell University Press, 1949.

Sanderson, William R. *Patent Your Invention and Make It Pay.* New York: Grosset & Dunlap, Inc., 1966.

In addition, the Small Business Administration in Washington, D.C., makes available the following pamphlets: *Know Your Patenting Procedures* and *Publications Available from the U.S. Patent Office.* The U.S. Patent Office, Washington, D.C., offers *Roster of Attorneys and Agents Registered to Practice before the U.S. Patent Office.* The Register of Copyrights, Library of Congress, Washington, D.C., offers *Copyright Law, Title 17, United States Code;* and *Copyrights and Copyright Office Services.*

Chapters 10 and 11

Baker, Robert A. *Help Yourself to Better Mail Order.* New York: Printer's Ink, 1953.

Banning, Douglas. *Techniques for Marketing New Products.* New York: McGraw-Hill Book Company, 1957.

Boyd, Harper W., Jr. *Contemporary American Marketing.* Homewood, Ill.: Richard Irwin Company, 1962.

Direct Marketing Magazine. Monthly. 224 Seventh Street, Garden City, Long Island, New York.

Graham, Irvin. *How to Sell through Mail Order.* New York: McGraw-Hill Book Company, 1949.

Guild, Walter. *How to Market Your Product Successfully.* New York: Prentice-Hall, Inc., 1955.

How to Win Success in the Mail Order Business. New York: Arco Publishing Company, Inc., 1955.

Jones, Manley. *The Marketing Process.* New York: Harper & Row, Publishers, 1965.

Lasser, J. K. *How to Run a Small Business.* New York: McGraw-Hill Book Company, 1955.

Lawyer, Kenneth, and Kelley, P. C. *How to Organize and Operate a Small Business.* Englewood Cliffs, N.J.: Prentice-Hall, Inc., 1955.

Mail Advertising Services Association Membership Roster. Washington, D.C.: Mail Advertising Agencies Association International, 1971.

Minrath, William R. *How to Run Your Own Business and Make It Pay.* New York: Van Nostrand Reinhold Company, 1955.

Stern, Alfred. *How Mail Order Fortunes Are Made.* Brooklyn, N.Y.: Selective Books, Inc., 1970.

Stone, Robert. *Successful Direct Mail Advertising and Selling.* Englewood Cliffs, N.J.: Prentice-Hall, Inc., 1955.

In addition, the Small Business Administration in Washington, D.C., makes available the following pamphlets: *How Trade Associations Help Small Business; Steps in Incorporating a Business; Checking Your Marketing Channels; Home Businesses: Mail Order Selling;* and *Selling by Mail with Limited Capital.* The U.S. Department of Commerce, Washington, D.C., offers *Establishing and Operating a Mail Order Business;* the Chamber of Commerce, Washington, D.C., offers *An Introduction to Doing Import and Export Business;* and the Superintendent of Documents, Washington, D.C., offers *Starting and Managing a Small Business of Your Own.*

Index